Voices
of
King Philip's War

Also by Faye George

———————————

Märchenhaft: Like a Fairy Tale, 2008

Back Roads, 2003

A Wound On Stone, 2001

Naming The Place: The Weymouth Poems, 1996
(chapbook)

*Only The Words, 1*995 (chapbook)

Voices
of
King Philip's War

Poems by Faye George

WordTech Editions

Published by WordTech Editions
P.O. Box 541106
Cincinnati, OH 45254-1106

ISBN: 9781625490032
LCCN: 2012954229

Poetry Editor: Kevin Walzer
Business Editor: Lori Jareo

Visit us on the web at www.wordtechweb.com

Cover portrait,
"King Philip: Metacom"
Original watercolor by Stephen F. Smalley, 2012

To those who carry the blood

Foreword

Voices of King Philip's War is an ambitious book. To tell the complicated story of the native peoples of New England in this conflict, and do it from beginning to end with such an unfaltering poetic voice, speaks volumes for Faye George's accomplishments as a writer. Her verse narrative does not stumble because her understanding of the interlinked tragedies of these indigenous peoples does not.

Faye George is a master tactician who knows how to keep the language of the poem moving forward without misstep, or lapse of verbal anticipation. And she has not hesitated to shake familiar words loose from their accepted moorings whenever the flow of the poem dictates such a loosening.

In literature, Americans know a great deal about the Plains Indians, but the story of the indigenous Woodland tribes of New England has not always been fully told. At stake was the survival of the people themselves, not so much as unincorporated individuals but as national peoples. Faye George tells the story marvelously in this collection. The book succeeds because she has dared to get into the minds of the actors themselves, giving them a voice that history has so long denied them.

—Ifeanyi Menkiti

Introduction

While the story of the Great Plains Indians has been well documented, their charismatic leaders enshrined in memory, their eloquent speeches preserved, their struggle popularly dramatized, the history of the Woodland cultures of New England has been largely ignored. The Algonquian nations of the east were effectively annihilated before the dominant White culture cared to record the intellectual and emotional experience of the people they displaced. It is my wish through the monologues, *Voices of King Philip's War,* to let these strong Indian (Native American) personalities speak their roles in the tragic drama of that war as passionately as I hear them above the muted pages of history.

This sequence of verse narratives has had a long gestation period. For most of my adult life I have been infatuated with the story of those defining days for the indigenous people of New England. I began assembling my own small library on the subject many years ago, gathering reprints of old texts, new histories as they appeared, and works on American Indian culture; a need for which I have no explanation beyond human sympathy. I am grateful to all whose scholarship has helped to inform the *Voices.*

Since the Woodland people of southern New England had no written language, we have only the occasional direct glimpse into their immediate thoughts from the few spare quotes preserved by colonial chroniclers. I have used italics to distinguish such directly quoted material. Events portrayed are taken from the historical record. The behaviors and attitudes of the personalities are presented as they appear to my imagination within the context of their respective roles in the war. The monologues are arranged, insofar as possible, to follow the war's progress. I have not included any civil or military colonial voices, as their thoughts and actions are for the most part well documented. The principal tribal groups represented in the monologues are Pokanoket/Wampanoag, Narragansett, Nipmuck, Mohegan, Niantic, and Pawtuckett/Pennacook.

There is much variation in seventeenth-century spelling; words and names vary widely among writers. This is especially true of phonetic approximations of Algonquian names, from which the modern writer must select at her own discretion. The early tracts may also contain conflicting and inaccurate accounts of events reiterated by subsequent writers. Much cross-checking among sources is necessary to avoid perpetuating errors and factual inconsistencies. Some areas of contention may never be adequately resolved.

Indian people commonly took new names to mark significant events in their lives. Sometime prior to, or shortly after, the death of Massasoit (Ousamequin), his sons approached the Plymouth authorities to receive English names. To honor and/or flatter the brothers, they were named for the Macedonian kings, Philip and his son Alexander The Great. The elder son, Wamsutta, Massasoit's successor as Great Sachem, was named "Alexander"; the younger, Metacom, in reverse chronology, became "Philip." However, Philip would succeed his brother as leader of the Wampanoag Federation within a year, upon Alexander's untimely and unexplained death.

I have used both the English, Philip, and the Indian, Metacom, interchangeably throughout the work.

. . . and History,
That always wants another telling,

Puts before us
The players, a choice of motives and their acts,

What was given, what received,
The facts or the presumed facts,

But omits the Chorus
Whose clear song extracts

From the furor of their passions
The truth of what is real.

—Daniel Hoffman, *Brotherly Love*

Table of Contents

Alexander: Wamsutta

Moonanam . . . Wamsutta . . . now Alexander,
    Chief Sachem.
As it was my father's—Massasoit's—wish
    That we should keep
The peace between us and the English,
    And as it was
Our custom to mark a death or other
    Solemn time
By shedding one's old name to take another,
    At his passing,
I, Wamsutta, with younger brother Metacom,
    Would ask that Plymouth
Bestow upon us English names, honoring
    Our father's wish.
Hence, I would now be known as "Alexander";
    My brother, "Philip":
Named for ancient kings, which flattered us as
    It was meant to do.
But keep the peace? I fear it was by then
    Too late for that.

I do not fault my father, so hard-pressed,
    The bargain made
To forge against the Narragansett threat
    An English shield,
With Wampanoag numbers so diminished
    By the plague
That swept our land like fire in autumn grass,
    Our flesh its kindling.
So many dead, the villages had no one left
    To bury them.

Their whited bones lay scattered over ground;
    Those who could, fled.
Crumbling wetus, grinning skulls, were left
    To greet the English,
Who found in our distress their lucky chance;
    Much as the bird
That lays its eggs in another bird's nest,
    Unwitting host,
Whose own offspring will be displaced by
    The invader's.
Caught between two wolves, my father thus
    Allied himself
With one against the other, believing
    English guns would
Help him keep encroaching Narragansetts
    At a distance.

He took a gambler's risk in trusting Whites,
    Knowing Englishmen
With little cause kill Indians; how some,
    Like Captain Hunt—
Who captured Epenow and Squanto—
    Would carry us
Away upon their ships to sell as slaves
    Beyond the sea.
But having cast his lot with Plymouth,
    My father's ears
Were closed to others' words, others' warnings.
    Edward Winslow
Came and went a welcome friend among
    The Pokanoket,
Which not a little troubled Corbitant,
    Pocasset Sachem,

A man of influence within the Federation,
    And not a little
Jealous, perhaps ambitious to become
    Chief Sachem.
Were Ousamequin—Massasoit—less loved
    Among the people,
It might have been the source of storms
    Between them.
For his part, Corbitant continued chary
    Of these English.
I see that Corbitant possessed a sense
    Of hidden things.
And had his hand been free to rally all
    The discontent,
The griefs that chafed and galled and vexed us,
    The injustices—
He would have rid us of the English before
    Another sun.
Before another Winslow or *his son*
    Would think himself
The master of these lands, and summon me—
    Summon me!
To answer at his bidding, where I go,
    Whence I come.

I answer thus this Englishman, trespasser
    Of Wampanoag land,
Reminding him, Josiah Winslow, how it was:
    —His father
Would not have lived to sire and raise him up
    Had it not been
The hand of Massasoit that lifted their distress
    In time of peril,

Giving succor to that wretched band
      Of castaways,
Landing pilgrimed on our shores in the worst
      Of winter frost.
None would have survived the famine time
      Without our corn,
Stolen Indian corn! —From corn to land,
      The theft goes on.
How is it that the suffered guest should come
      To rule the house?

Summon me? —Wamsutta, Alexander,
      Chief Sachem
Of the Wampanoag Federation!
      I give my answer:
Not for this did my father and our people,
      With all good will,
Give yours a place to make their homes
      And dwell among us;
Not to submit as slaves to English law,
      Not to live as
Children of the English governor!
      Now you hear this:
We are not your children, neither your slaves.
      Nor will you,
Josiah Winslow, tell me how I shall
      Dispose my land.
Do not send your soldiers, armed and dressed
      Like plated beasts,
To fetch me thither with a pointed gun.
      Do not wave your
Paper treaties made of lies before my face.
      And do not force my hand!

King Philip: Metacom

I am a bone in the teeth of two dogs:
    Submission? or War?
They chew and chew until one of them must
    Swallow me whole.
With my brother's death, I, Philip, Metacom,
    The second son,
Must carry this long struggle on alone.
    As sachem now,
With little time to mourn, I fear the turn
    Of things to come.

The English came here poor, forlorn, distressed,
    A piteous handful.
My father, Massasoit, befriended them,
    Provided aid.
He taught them all the needed skills they lacked,
    To fish, hunt game;
What streams the alewives follow in the spring,
    How to catch eels,
That burying a fish beneath the corn
    Makes it grow sweet. . . .
Thus they survived and prospered well beyond;
    Then others came.
There followed more and more, with more to come.
    What had we here?
My father's counselors spoke out in alarm:
    "Destroy them now!
Pull their fences down that snake along like
    Serpents over ground
To stay the passage of our moccasins
    North, east, south, west.

We are as captive now as their milk cows!"
    My father calmed them.
And having in his heart no wish for war,
    Thus it went on
Until my aging father felt his years,
    And moving on. . . .
Wamsutta, elder brother, as Sachem
    Alexander,
Would join him in the spirit world before
    Another snow,
Once taken into custody—Winslow's gun
    Beneath his chin.
Some things they would question him to learn,
    Whence all sudden
Great sickness strikes him down; he dies before
    We get him home.
If truth be known, it is my strong belief
    They poisoned him.
Oh, it burns, this thought, live coal in the heart
    That wants revenge!
By passion pressed, by reason stopped: revenge
    At what price bought?

The way of English justice has two paths:
    Straight for Englishman,
For Indian it twists and bends, the snake's
    Own crooked way.
Let twenty honest Indians testify
    Who speak the truth,
It is as nothing to the English court;
    If there be one bad,
Lying Indian to say what pleases them,
    His word is taken.

What means this word the English say we are:
    "Salvage . . . savage"?
Some less thing than men like them, who keep
    One house, one place,
One town to be all year, and cut up land like
    Side of beef for this.
The Indian way, *savage* way, better for us,
    Better for Earth!
What did we know, what could we know of
    Men such as these?
We took their beads and trinkets and were pleased
    To have these gifts,
Even as the English knew that we knew not
    What we gave up
For this they offered in exchange for land:
    Coats, kettles, cloth,
The iron hoes, but most we wanted guns.
    And so we lost
Much of the skill our fathers had to hunt
    With bow and arrow.
We grew more and more dependent, trading
    With the English.
The worst of them will feed our people rum,
    Make fools of them.
And they despise us for it, use us ill,
    Impose on us
The laws that fine and punish should we scorn
    Their stubborn will.
They tell us now we must not hunt or fish
    On Sabbath Day.
And thus they sweep away our right of birth
    To live as Indians,
Proud and free as the Master Of All life
    Has made us.

Never again! Never again such insult
    As Plymouth
Put on me at Taunton! Never again
    Humiliation,
Forced confession: *Naughtiness of my heart. . . .*
    Never again
Will I surrender my weapons to them;
    Never again
Give cause to one of my own to turn on me,
    Calling out as he left,
For all to hear—*white-livered cur!*
    No, never again!
That slur—the blade of it stuck in my heart
    These four long years.

The young bloods ready to attack at whim
    Do not understand,
First we must plan this, and I fear I am
    Losing them.
Daily it gets worse, and we are not yet
    Ready to act.
With Plymouth pushing us past the limits
    Of patience,
How do I keep their respect as long as
    I hold them back?

Much as the weed that sprouts among the corn
    Goes first unnoticed,
Then all at once the pest beneath your nose
    Has multiplied,
Is it now between us and the English.
    Take heed, my friend,
The weeds grow thick on Pokanoket land.
    So many weeds

They must in time expand along the wind's
        Long-fingered reach.
Everything is not enough for them:
        They want our land,
They want us gone—and more—they want us
        Never to have been!

And have we not, in truth, helped make it so?
        The ancient quarrels:
Indian against Indian, sagamore
        And sachem;
Pequot against Narragansett against
        Wampanoag. . . .
We have been like seabirds fighting for
        A scrap of clam,
While another, seeing his advantage,
        Comes swooping in
And scoops it up from under them; just so
        The English use
Our quarrels against us and they prosper.
        As single strands
Of hemp will snap beneath slight weight but
        Woven in a cord
Can bear great loads, must we unite and rid
        Ourselves of them:
One heart, one mind, one body in this cause.
        A great storm of us,
A mighty warrior wind, the hurricane
        That sweeps the land,
Whose fierce power bends all unto its will.
        So must we gather,
All tribes together, lay our plan with care,
        Stealth and cunning,

The time, the place to strike that best will serve
    The promised end.
But let us keep the peace that is, such as
    It is . . . till then.
For now, cool down the blood and hide the rage
    Behind the eye.
It will not do to light the fire before
    The wood is dry.

The scribe, John Sassamon, would force my hand;
    I cannot trust him.
His service comes most dear, takes much watching;
    "Cowaunckamish:
My service to you, my Sachem*,"* he says
    With his false tongue,
Then goes behind my back and does me wrong.
    Dissemblers all,
These Praying Indians, who learn to lie,
    To spy, betray. . . .
It was my great mistake to have him close,
    So faithless did
He show himself in writing out my Will,
    To put it so
My land and goods would all be left to *him*—
    Not wife and son?
His Christian schooling split him heart from tongue.
    He makes his way
In the wind that drives me to the precipice,
    Carrying tales to
Winslow's ears, betraying his own blood for
    Those who oppress us,
Whose schools make dupes and fools of Indians.
    For John Eliot

And his gospel, I care less than for—
        A button!
He learns our language not to learn our hearts
        But to confuse,
Corrupt our thoughts, and turn us from the path
        Great Spirit has
Revealed to us, to know and wisely use
        The gifts of Earth
And learn her wisdom. John Eliot knows
        Nothing but his Book;
Deaf to the lessons of our songs, our prayers,
        The many-tongued
Voices of Earth that speak to him who has
        It in his heart
To listen to the whisper of the moss as to
        The cry of the wind,
To sniff the air and breathe *it* in—*the god,*
        The god of this!
Thus has the Master Of Life made Indians,
        Made us—his children.

The Massachusetts governor sends his man
        To summon me
To sign another treaty, but this time—
        This time I answer:
Your governor is but a subject of
        King Charles.
I shall not treat with him, a subject.
        I treat of peace with
The king, my brother, only; when he comes,
        I am ready.
Let them know forthwith, here too there walks
        A man of worth,

A man of office: sachem, king—Indian!
    These high English
Think to rule unchecked as masters here,
    Take all we have,
All we are: our honor, our pride of spirit.
    Oh, it is clear
There can be no justice for the Indian
    Without war.

Knowing now the lay of the land, I will
    Feed their lust with
Every rod of earth that I have left to trade
    For powder and guns,
And ransom it back with the blood and bones
    Of them. For myself,
I, Philip, Metacom, Pometacomet,
    Oh listen, friend—
Before the English tongue shall speak the law
    To Indians,
Before the English hand shall rule me with
    A scratching pen,
Before the English foot shall grind my rights
    To Plymouth sand—hear me:
I am determined not to live until
    I have no country.

John Sassamon

To be John Sassamon, know the Whiteman's God,
    And teach His will
To other Indians as I have learned it,
    Is to be loved
By Christian, despised by pagan brethren.
    A Praying Indian
Is neither fox nor hare, belonging nowhere,
    Save for my skills
Learned under English tutelage, which serve me
    To advantage.
Though not without regret at what divides me
    From the people.
Have I not been asked, *What are you, Indian
Or Englishman?*
The Pequot got his answer from my gun's
    Well-spoken mouth.
Near two score years have past since the attack
    On Mystic Fort,
And not a day has passed I do not ask
    Myself the same.

Yet I must make the best of things that are
    Now as they are.
And if as I suspect it is that Philip
    Prepares for war,
The governor must know before the first
    Shot of the gun
That such is planned, and Sassamon has proved
    A faithful Christian
Who stands with him, at peril of life, against
    The Sachem.

Should Philip learn it was the scribe's loose tongue
    Gave the alarm,
You may count the days—nay—hours until the end
    Of Sassamon.
These troubled times we circle one another
    Warily
When our paths cross; I fear he reads my thoughts,
    As I read his.
 Oh, I must be very careful, I am sure
    That I am watched.

William Nahauton

My name, Nahauton, the English never spell
    The same way twice.
I have a brother, Anthony, but I,
    I am William,
The one they called to testify of what
    Perhaps I knew.
I could not say I saw with my own eyes
    The deed as done.
The little that I knew, I told it as Patuckson
    Told to me,
That he was standing on a hill most near to
    Assawompsett Pond,
Where he could see them, Mattashunannamo,
    Tobias and
His son, and swears upon the Book they did so
    Murder Sassamon
And poke his body through the ice that it
    Should seem he drowned.
I am, like the deceased, a Christian Indian,
    And I do pray
His soul may be at rest with Christ our Lord
    In heaven.

The facts about a gambling debt are vague,
    But what I heard
Is that Patuckson lost his coat to one
    Of the accused
And, being loath to pay the debt he owed,
    Made up his story.
I pray that these who hanged did not so die
    From perjury.

With all the doubt surrounding this sad case,
    One thing is certain,
Philip will not take this trespass calmly.
    Tobias served
The Sachem as a valued counselor;
    It could mean war.

I know the Indian mind, and I know Philip
    Will see this as
A challenge to his own authority.
    He must as well
Concern himself with holding back his
    Angry braves,
Who seethe with—as they see it—every new
    Indignity.
They press him to take up the tomahawk
    And strike—strike now.
He must save face or lose his status as
    Their sachem.
I think he's buying time. And buying guns
    As well, I hear.
The rumors fly, and so it does appear
    That Philip
Travels more and more from Pokanoket
    To the Nipmuck,
And his old enemies the Narragansett. . . .
    He covers ground,
So to draw the tribes together and drive
    The English out.
The talk is, powwaws warn it will go bad
    For Wampanoags
If Philip's men be first in spilling blood.
    Thus far small bands

Content themselves with staging petty raids
    On homes and barns,
Stealing here a pig, there a cow, hoping
    To provoke
Some Englishman to be the one who fires
    The shot that counts.
If war must come, if it be God's will,
    May heaven help us all!

Awashonks

The council fire was lit at Pokanoket
   And I, Awashonks,
Squaw Sachem of Sakonnet, called there
   By Philip,
Hastened hence to take my place at Montaup.
   Never had I
Seen at once so many angry Indians
   All come together
In one place, and to be as it seemed
   All of one mind.
We gathered round, intent to listen close
   As Sachem Philip
Recited one by one the English wrongs;
   And with each wrong
Put down a stick and when the pile had grown
   He then took up
A flaming brand and set the sticks afire,
   And bid us rise
And put our hearts into the dance that calls
   An Indian to war.
Then louder than the shrillest *Hai-ya, hi-ya*
   Of the dance,
My voice above the tom-tom cried for war.
   But coming back,
Once in Sakonnet, found my passion cooled,
   The fever gone.

It was about this time that Captain Church,
   My English neighbor,
Well-armed with rum, tobacco, and all his
   Courtly charm,

Paid me a visit, with some questions posed
  By indirection,
Tucked in among much flattery, by which
  He hoped to coax
Out where my sympathies would lie if it
  Should come to war;
Reminding me I had some years before
  By signed agreement
Submitted to the Plymouth government,
  And thus its law.
And so when Philip heard no more from me
  He grew concerned
Enough to send his messengers to learn
  How things now stood.
The time had come to parley, thus we would
  Meet in council,
His warriors and mine, and speak our thoughts.
  But I was shrewd,
For unbeknownst to these foresaid, I sent
  For Captain Church.
He came, and with another Englishman.
  At first I did not
See them there against the trees, where they
  Stood watching me—
Hard at the dance and all a-sweat as I was—
  Like men still young
In eyes, who for the first brave time behold
  A woman.

When I broke free to greet the Captain, then
  I let it out,
Just what was in the message Philip sent:
  That I must join

In making war against the English or,
    As their houses
And their cattle were attacked, they'd think
    Sakonnet did it.
He'd fix it so the blame would fall on me
    For all the mischief.
Thus in the telling I upturned the pot
    And spoiled the stew
The Great Chief had so craftily brewed up.
    The Pokanokets' eyes
Narrowed down to smoldering slits and fixed
    On me their scorch.
Then it was that Captain Church espied the
    Cache of bullets
They carried in their bags. And what was their
    Intended use?
The knaves gave saucy answer, they were
    For shooting pigeons.

And did a lively scene ensue when Church
    Spoke up and said
I should put my trust in Plymouth and knock
    Them on the head.
This set off a murmuring and my own
    Counselor, Little Eyes,
Who chafed, instead, to knock the doughty Captain
    On the head,
Hatched such a plan to get the man alone,
    And would have done it
Had not more sober warriors stayed his hand.
    And with the Captain
Not a man to quail before a threat, 'twas
    Time to end it.

When later I saw Weetamoo, she lowered
    Her vixen eyes,
And smiled the way that women do when
    Signaling,
I understand, I have my secrets, too.
    And then she said,
"I do suspect our clever Captain Church
    Did get to you."
"What might it be would make you it think so?"
    I gave reply,
With something of a sneer, knowing her mind.
    She answered that
He'd tried his charm on her, implying I
    Had been seduced
By the English Captain's winning ways.
    Not so! Not so!
Nor would I let King Philip fence me round,
    I sharply told her,
It was my way to keep an open mind;
    If war must come,
I would go where best it served my people,
    And I did not
Intend to find myself at last upon
    The losing end.

Church planned to come again, or so he said,
    To have my answer,
Whether we be on the side of Plymouth
    Or of Philip.
But like a lightning flash the war began
    And swept us up,
So many of my warriors gone to Philip,
    I followed on.

Whatever may be said, we are not cowards,
      We Sakonnets.
Nor are we fools; we gave the cause our best,
      We suffered much:
The winter—cold, hungry, hunkered down
      In Nipmuck country.
So many dead, so many others sick,
      So many
Slipped away to join the English and betray
      The rest of us.
I saw the cause was lost, though Philip
      To the last would not.
I saw the only chance to keep my head
      Upon my neck
Would be to sue for peace, and so I did.
      And so I should—
To spare my people further suffering.
      No, it was not
What gossips said, that Benjamin Church
      Had turned my head.

Ninigret

He must be strong and quick who strikes
    The hornet's nest.
And I am old now: old eyes, old ears, old bones,
    This tortoise skin.
Ninigret no longer wields the hatchet;
    I stand apart.
If you would fight the English, you go talk
    To Canonchet.
I hear his Narragansetts have been
    Sharpening the stick,
That Metacom, Philip, goes there often
    And moves freely
In his village. Narragansett, Wampanoag
    Are as brothers,
Old enmities forgot, of one mind joined
    In single aim:
Drive the English back beyond the sea
    To their own land,
Reclaim the high ground lost to us when
    The Whiteman came
With his god and his law to make us powerless
    Under him.

These shrewd and cunning English laws are snares
    Contrived to catch
And find us guilty by their say-so . . .
    Of who knows what?
The winter that I spent among the Dutch
    With the Monhatoes,
Taking physic for my health, caused such concern
    Among the English,

That on return I must answer to an
        Inquisition—
Of some conspiracy, some hostile act
        They conjured up:
Perhaps I'm plotting—with the French, the Dutch?
        No end of ways
They find to trouble us; they interfere
        In what the tribes
Between themselves should settle with no
        English hand put in.
Then charge up the expense of it, whatever
        They demand in
Wampum, furs, or land: a clever trick that
        Keeps us in their debt.
One must be ever mindful of the traps
        They set for us.

Huh! It makes me laugh when their preachers come
        To make of us
Good Christian men like them. Oh, I told him,
        Mr. Mayhew,
"You first go make the English good, then you
        Come preach to me."
They cannot much agree among themselves
        How all should worship;
It seems each Christian has a different god,
        And all at war.

I am no more the English friend than Philip;
        I wish them gone,
But have lived long enough to know how few
        Brave words and
Noble thoughts well spoken at the council fire
        Will meet success

When acted on. It is a reckless scheme that
      Promises to bring
Worse troubles on our heads. What chance have we
      Against the English?
The time is past to act the bear, for we
      Have lost our claws.
In dealing with the Whiteman now, one must
      Play the fox.
They are too many and too strong for us.
      I want no part
In this adventure: Niantic people
      Will be neutral.
Such is my wish; that is the counsel I give
      As sachem,
For my warriors to heed and follow.
      Those who go with
The English, or to the swamps with Philip,
      Go without me.

I have seen my day, have sung the war song,
      Taken blows, and
At my best when young paid out twice as many
      To my enemies.
The snows of many years are on my head,
      And stored within
A wisdom learned: sometimes to get ahead
      It's best to stay behind.
I keep my counsel and avoid entanglements
      As much as possible.

Before this ends the English may be pressed
      To use my agency.
And I may have to send a Wampanoag head
      Or two to Boston

To prove I have not joined in Philip's war.
  I hear it has
Been published since, the governor will pay
  In coats for heads.

And I would bet my own good English coat
  Old Uncas now
Will jump with his Mohegans to the right side
  Of the English.
They will use him as their ready man, their
  Trusted Indian.
Their fawning pet, liar, maker of mischief,
  The worst among us:
A black-hearted wretch with the tongue
  Of a snake.
When there is dirty work to do in service
  Of the English,
You can count on Uncas; he it was killed
  Miantonomo,
Yet kept the ransom paid out for his life.
  When Commissioners
At Hartford gave their secret blessing
  For the killing,
He carried out the task with lustful pleasure,
  Cutting the flesh
From the Sachem's still warm shoulder, saying
  As he ate it,
It was the sweetest meal he ever eat; it made
  Him have strong heart.

I think of that and, no, I would not so wish
  To end my days.
Nor like Sassacus, his Pequots massacred.
  That great nation,

28

Whose warriors once ranged the land with none
      To challenge them,
Whose very name could chill the heart of
      Enemy or friend.
Yet before the sun had time to rise and
      Warm the day,
Their day was done; the massacre at Mystic
      Would spare neither
Warrior, nor squaw, nor helpless papoose—
      No mercy—none!
Too late the warning: *Wanux! Wanux!*
      Englishmen! Englishmen!
The soldiers had their orders—slay them all!
      And slay they did.
Those who did not die by sword or gun,
      Would perish roasting
In the flames of burning wetus. —That too
      Was Uncas' victory!
And in the iron *Wanux* fist, a lesson
      For the rest of us.

Uncas

You hear many bad things about Uncas.
     And I know who
The Indians are would say them: Canonchet,
     Ninigret, Philip . . .
Enemies all much jealous of Uncas.
     They say Uncas
Lusts for power: Uncas turned on Sassacus,
     His wife's own father,
Uncas helped the English destroy the
     Pequot Nation;
Uncas killed the Narragansett Sachem,
     Slew Miantonomo
In service of the English. Oh, yes,
     Naughty Uncas!
Maybe you don't know we were at war when
     This thing happened.
So I capture him and the English say,
     You take him but—
No torture. And I see what they want is
     To be rid of him,
But not by English hand: they have Uncas
     —Hatchet man.

They lie who say for English friendship I
     Betray our people.
Any bad thing that you can think, you hear
     How Uncas did it.
They say of me I stole another man's wife;
     A thing not true!
I never hold Obechiquod's squaw to keep
     Against her will.

And—"Uncas tortures enemies!"—Oh, yes,
    You will hear it.
Did I torture my worst enemy—Miantonomo?
    —No!
My brother knocks him on the head, one blow,
    And that was that.
What you heard—the Narragansetts said—
    How I cut a piece
Of flesh from off his shoulder and I ate it. . . .
    Yes, that is so.
But here is something maybe you don't know:
    I paid to him
An honor when I said it was sweet and it
    Made my heart strong.
Indians have some customs like that, maybe
    You should know.

I ask him why he not entreat me so
    To spare his life,
As in his place I would myself have done.
    And maybe then
I would have let him go. But this proud Sachem
    Does not speak,
He keeps his tongue in tight behind his teeth;
    Miantonomo
Must show he rather die than beg his life
    Of Uncas.

You listen, and let Uncas tell you what:
    Miantonomo,
Ninigret—many times, many ways they
    Try to kill me:
By ambush, by poison, by witchcraft. . . .
    My English friends

31

Look out for me, so I look out for them
    When they need help
To maybe save their house and barn and cows,
    And even scalp,
From Indians who want to drive them out.
    As in this fight
With Philip, Mohegans help the English put
    Quick end to him.
Then Mohegan, English, everyone have peace,
    Live all good friends.

When the governor have me answer him this
    Rumor he has heard:
Uncas hides Pequots, says they are Mohegans,
    I say my heart
Is hurt if he would so believe this thing of me.
    To him I say:
This heart is not mine, it is yours. I have
    No men; they are all yours.
Command me any hard thing;
    I will do it.
I will not believe any Indians' words
    Against the English.
If any man shall kill an Englishman,
    I will put him
To death, were he never so dear to me.
    He liked it well,
The good speech that I made him, and gave to me
    A fair red coat.

To deal with Englishmen, an Indian
    Needs two tongues.
You watch Uncas, I always know just where
    To stand, which tree

To look behind, no matter if in Boston
      Or the swamps.
I keep this finger to the wind, this ear
      To the ground,
Pay attention, take in information:
      Know what goes on
Is many times more useful than hundred
      Belt of wampum.

Quaiapen

Quaiapen—Magnus, Sunk Squaw, the Old Queen—
    Tells you this. Listen!
I was there—yes, *there,* at the great walled fort
    When soldiers struck.
The soldiers came with flaming brands,
    Firing the wetus!
Thrusting them within—*Whoosh!*— The old,
    The sick, the children. . . .
I will not forget—not ever forget—the smell,
    The searing stench
Of burning flesh, and everywhere I look—
    Yotaanit,
Many-clawed bird of fury, merciless,
    Burning, burning,
Treeward-leaping, dancing, flying—here—there,
    All-consuming.

The fire—a wind, a wave, a roar, a writhing
    Scream of terror!
Shriveled scream of gasping throats, choking,
    Drinking fire—
Swallowed in fire, its crackling, yellow teeth;
    Its savage mouth
Spitting smoke, blinding, over-spreading smoke,
    And those you love
Engulfed. —*Yotaanit,* the many-clawed,
    The merciless!
Your feet are stones, you have no power to run.
    You hear the guns,
The bullets whiz, you open to the mercy
    Of the guns.

When someone—I know not who it was,
    Canonchet?
Quinnapin? . . . took my hand in his and said,
    "Come follow me,"
And led me through the smoke to Weetamoo.
    "Take care of her,"
I barely heard through the smoke, the din
    As we ran—
Tried to run, stumbling on frozen ground.
    And it was snowing then.

The English way of war proved as I feared:
    Kill, kill, kill!
And leave no living thing. So was it at
    The Pequot fort,
When to our lasting shame and haunting grief
    The Narragansett
Had some hand in it; that which was done
    At Mystic Fort
To Sassacus comes back upon our heads
    In kind this day.

Like English cows that chew and chew and chew,
    We've sucked the rind
Of enmity, fed old quarrels anew. —And
    How did this begin
That Indians kill Indians in service
    Of the English?
Do Whites kill Whites for us? —Huh! They all
    Unite against us.

Even Roger Williams, the Englishman
    Most trusted by us,

Who wished to know our ways and speak with us
    In our own tongue,
Who wrote our words, their spoken sounds, made
    A little book of them—
Even he, who knew us best, who many nights
    Did lodge with us,
The gentle Whiteman whom Canonicus,
    Great Sachem,
Father of my husband, called *netop*: his *friend*.
    And gave him land
And made him welcome here among us,
    When his own people
Cast him out and drove him off from them.
    —Even he, at last,
Would join these thankless same, his countrymen,
    When called by them,
Against the Indian friends who called him *brother*,
    Who trusted him.

My brother, Ninigret, would take no stand
    Against the English.
Ninigret is politic, he hopes his
    Small canoe
Can take him through the whirlpool, the storm
    That swirls about us.
This brother is another man from him
    Who one time spoke
In bold defiance of the Colonies,
    How he would war
With Uncas, have his head, and should the English
    Thwart him in it,
Would turn on them, *kill and heap their cattle*
    Up as high as

English wetus, nor would an Englishman
  Be safe to stir
From out his door to piss, for fear he meet
  His death.

But Ninigret is crafty, "serpent wise,"
  Some say of him.
Brother, sister, we see our duty each with
  Different eyes.
Many words have passed between us
  On the subject.
What he will or will not do, oh, perhaps
  The gods may know.
What I know is, if each tribe seek its own
  Small end in this,
The moment's gain shall be the morrow's loss
  For all of us.

Blood is on their hands, Narragansett blood,
  Innocent blood,
Shed unprovoked at Great Swamp Fort, as once
  At Sachem's Plain.
No, we do not forget our valiant kinsman,
  Miantonomo,
The cruel betrayal. Let his spirit be
  At last avenged!
My warriors and Canonchet's are all
  With Metacom.
The English no more doubt the way of it,
  Have they not struck?
How can we longer feign neutrality,
  Such punishment
As they have put on us for sheltering
  Wampanoags?

We are not to be crushed at whim like ants
    Beneath the foot!
They shall find these ants have a mighty sting
    When stepped upon.
Let them learn, like the foolish man struck down
    By the tree he fells,
That they shall not escape the long reach
    Of their victim.
My warriors have sworn revenge; they vow
    To fight as long
As they have breath, and kill two Englishmen
    For every loved one
Lost to us. Oh, I see no way back, nor
    Would I wish it.
To be an English dog is not for one
    Born Indian,
No less a queen thought wise by birth and years
    Among her people.

The powwaws meet and murmur, make offerings
    Of tobacco,
The sacred *wuttamauog,* read the smoke breath
    Of the spirits,
Seek their counsel, protection in this peril,
    Ask their wisdom.
What wisdom now, what comfort do I bring
    In this travail
To these my people, who must flee with me
    Like hunted beasts?
We are as leaves in the teeth of the storm,
    Torn from the tree,
Blown hither and yon, but to crumble back
    To earth at last.

If the courage of the young is to venture
      At whatever cost,
The courage of the old is to endure
      When all is lost.
Blood is on the horizon, yonder comes
      The fierce dawn.

Canonchet: Nanuntenoo

They do me honor who confuse me with
    My father.
Miantonomo was the man I, Canonchet,
    Would wish to be,
A man well known among good men for his
    Highmindedness,
The one Canonicus would choose to lead
    The Narragansett
As chief sachem when his own years at last
    Were counted up.
I carry in my heart the bleeding wound
    Of his betrayal.
The Commissioners at Hartford, who handed
    Him to Uncas
In secret for the killing, shall be forever
    Shadowed with shame.
As an oak is to a mushroom, was he
    To that Mohegan!

They came to treat of peace with sword in hand,
    Our English friends.
A sham, not peace but forced submission,
    Contrived to
Keep us helpless under them; a paper peace
    Cast to the wind
When Philip's men struck Swansea and every
    Indian patriot
Cheered them on. And so between the tribes
    A new and stronger
Brotherhood of blood was born that Philip
    Fathered in us.

Yet not every Narragansett was as
    Ready as the next
To join the Wampanoags in this war.
    We met in council,
Whether to follow Ninigret's lead and
    Wait it out or
Take the greater risk for the greatest good:
    Our freedom.
When the powwaw's time to speak had come,
    He raised his eyes,
And one by one the old man took us in
    And then began:
How in a vision he had seen two eagles
    From their perch
High on a cliff swoop down upon a school
    Of spawning fish,
When foaming white on white a great wave struck
    And swept the pair
Beneath the water, not to rise again;
    Nor feather nor claw,
Nothing was seen, as if no bird had been.
    So ill an omen
Excited many fears and murmurings.
    And thus I spoke:
"I wear the eagle feather, like my father.
    Like him, I prize
My honor above all and I will fight
    The Whites who strive
To take from us both home and honor—
    I will fight them!
I have no fear of water or of signs
    The powwaws see.
Let that high one who sets the sun in place,
    Who makes the storms,

Who sends the rain, the snows in season,
    Whose hidden thoughts
No man may know, he who made me prince,
    And my father
Sachem before me, let him keep his counsel
    And work his will.
I shall never surrender. I shall fight,
    If I must—to the death!"

The treaty signed in Boston, I but signed
    To buy more time.
Never would I honor terms demanding
    We deliver over
Every Wampanoag in our care—
    A coat for each!
An offer made to tempt us with compliance:
    One head, one coat.
Two if brought alive; alive they make good
    Profit sold for slaves.
What price an Indian's life? For Philip's head,
    Why—twenty coats,
And twice that number paid to him who brings
    Him in alive.
I held my tongue and took their gift—their bribe,
    A coat—what else!
A fine cloth coat laced round with silver thread.
    The time would come
Ere long when I could speak my mind and say
    What then I must
Choke down—how I despised them all and scorned
    Their bad-faith treaties
Signed against my will in bitter falsehood.
    I took my leave,

Returning to my country to prepare
    For what would come.

Free at last to speak out strong the anger
    In my heart
When next they sent a messenger from Boston,
    This I told him:
We did not take our war canoes across
    The great salt sea
And set our wetus up in your king's land,
    As you have done,
You English, saying your high god has sent you
    To rule over us.
No! No! Your praying men that tell you this,
    They tell you wrong.
The Master Of All Life has put us here
    To rule ourselves.
He set us on the Earth here in this place,
    This ground, this land:
Indians' land, born here of our Earth Mother,
    Whose green breast grows
The beans, squash, corn—and brings the animals
    That nourish us.
When first you came, you English bargained for
    Our beaver pelts,
And then you bargained for our land, and now—
    —And now you want
To trade with me for Wampanoag lives.
    I give my answer:
"Tell the governor—tell your chief men who much
    Like to make treaties—
I will deliver up no Wampanoag.
    Not so much as

The paring of a Wampanoag's nail!
    —You tell them that!"

We did not seek this bloody war, it was
    Thrust upon us
Where we hoped to winter-over far removed
    From conflict.
In the time of long cold nights, before the
    Wolf Moon takes the sky,
They struck at Great Swamp Fort in the heart of
    Our country.
The fort planned out and built by Stonewall John,
    Who walled it high
With poles, enclosing many hundred wetus,
    And these well stocked
With food, dried fish and meat, and stores of corn;
    The work most done
Before the trees had dropped their leaves, save for
    One opening.
Through this they came, guided by the captive,
    Indian Peter.
They would punish us for heeding not their
    Bribes and threats.
They came well armed, Moseley, Church, Winslow
    First among them.
My warriors, better than a match for
    English soldiers,
Would have destroyed them all, had we not
    So soon used up
The powder and shot, and with it all advantage.
    They fired the wetus,
Killing scores of women, children, old ones.
    All who could, fled,

Escaping to the cold and frozen swamp;
      Fire took the rest.

And with them went the stores of meat and corn
      To last the winter.
I vowed to make them pay for this: life for life.
      —I swore it.
Let them reap in their home fields the killing
      They have sown.
The fire they brought, I would send back,
      Gift of Canonchet.
Let them taste it—their houses set aflame,
      As were our homes,
With the helpless in them: babies at the breast,
      The old, the lame. . . .
This was war, war fought to the death—war that
      Makes the heart a hatchet.

Had Philip won the Mohawks to our cause,
      Had they but turned
As viciously upon the English as on him,
      We could have
Driven out the Whites and freed our country.
      Yes, if only. . . .
We had our victories and they were sweet,
      If bitter-sweet;
Each victory had its cost in those lives lost
      That purchased it.
Nipmuck, Wampanoag, Narragansett
      Together fought
At Quabaug, Nashaway, Quinsigamond
      Squakeag, Agawam,
Squinshepauke, Squinnicook, Wessagusset. . . .
      And west into

Connecticut, from Simsbury to Plymouth's
    Garrisons we struck.
Providence would burn, but for past kindnesses
    No harm come to
Roger Williams, though Narragansetts speak
    Strong words to him:
You have driven us out of our own country,
    And then pursued us
To our great misery, and your own, and we are
    Forced to live upon you.

The food the soldiers burnt up in the fort
    Proved every day
More precious. If they could not catch us,
    They would starve us,
Laying waste our fields: there would be no
    Harvest for us.
And for our part we raided homes and barns,
    And when we could
Drove cattle off and feasted on the flesh,
    But most survived
As best they could on groundnuts, roots, and acorns.
    This scavenging
Would not keep us alive for long, I knew;
    For as we watched
The Hunger Moon grow full in its cold sky,
    The people withered.
If any would survive, we must prepare
    For planting time.

I met with Philip, who agreed we plant
    At Squakeag
In the spring, but would need the cache
    Of seed corn

Hidden underground at Wannamoisett.
      The plan: I would
Return, retrieve the seed and send it on,
      While I remained
To take the war back to the doors of Plymouth.
      I set out from
Wachusett with my party, stopping at
      Pawtucket Falls
To make our camp where fish were plentiful.
      And when my scouts
Were seen by Captain Pierce, he, innocent
      Of our true numbers,
Took the bait as set and followed us into
      A deadly ambush.
I will say the Captain fought most bravely
      Till he fell.
We came in surrounding them and slaying all,
      Which gave us heart.
But proved a short-lived victory, the way
      A false spring warmth
Calls forth the bud that meets the killing frost:
      Thus it was for us.

So soon were we discovered in our camp,
      Led on by those,
The false, the faint of heart, who would betray
      Us all when caught.
As I fled across the stream, my quick foot slipped,
      My gun went in,
Now wet and useless as a rotten stick—
      All spirit died in me.
I felt upon my shoulder the hand of
      My pursuer

And knew it for the bony hand of death,
  Cold death, my death.
But worse, the death in *him*—an Indian—
  Of pride of race.
I turned and saw in his bronze face the lost
  Eyes of the slave;
No freer was my captor than an English
  Hunting hound.
I gave him my wet gun, and sitting down
  Upon a stone,
Waited for his master—an Englishman—
  To claim his prize,
The prince his slave had caught by luck for him
  In this hot chase.
A soldier, green young sapling, first to come
  Approach me,
You much child, I tell him, *no understand*
  Matters of war.
Let your brother or your chief come, him
  I will answer.

Captain Denison would offer me my life
  If I would then
Desert the cause and turn my back on Philip—
  I scoff at him,
"Let me hear no more of this, Denison,
  You insult me.
I was born a prince, my honor *is* my life,
  So kill me!
I like it well, then I shall die before
  My heart is soft
Or I have said any thing unworthy
  Of myself."

Oweneco

My father killed his father, now the same
     Comes round again:
Oweneco's hand, hand of Uncas' son,
     Kills Canonchet.
By his own spoken wish it is that one
     Of equal rank,
A prince by birth as he, and no man less,
     Should take his life.
Much proud, as in his father's way, he will
     Ask no mercy.
He *like it well*, he say: better he die
     Than he betray.
Captain Denison brings him prisoner here
     To Stonington,
With order I must have all friendly Indians
     Share as brothers
Some part the glory of destroying one
     So great a prince.
War not end with him, he say. You great rogue,
     I tell him. And so
He shed his coat and bare his chest in scorn
     For us to shoot him.
It's Pequots do the shooting, Mohegans
     Cut the head off
And quarter up his parts, Niantics
     Burn them up.
The head we take to Hartford to show our
     Faithfulness.

With Canonchet dead, his people lose heart:
     Sick and hungry,

No gunpowder left, no spirit to fight with.
    We tell soldiers,
Follow us for good success, Indians know
    What swamps where
Indians go hide in. —We do good work
    At Nipsachuck,
Kill many Narragansetts: easy victory
    For Major Talcott.

Good news for him we shoot the Old Queen,
    Quaiapen,
He calls *piece of venom.* —Same time bring in
    Stonewall John.
I tell the Major, this one, you no shoot him,
    Mohegans want
This prisoner, have some fun, make him dance;
    They durst not refuse.
I know their thoughts: *Humm,* what these "savages"
    Will do to prisoner. . . .
The Major, his soldiers, all good Christian men,
    But you know what?
These good Christian men much eager to watch,
    See the big man,
Stonewall John, how he suffer torture.
    This Narragansett
Who builds big fort, house, walls, all everything,
    Not do much when
We be through with him, lop fingers first, then toes.
    Make him dance,
Make him sing—hands, feet, all bloody—ask him,
    Narragansett,
How does he like to make war upon us now?
    He sneers at us,

Will not cry out, not show he suffer much.
      He boasts he once
Killed nineteen Englishmen, and gun still charged,
      Finding not one more,
He shoots Mohegan: make even twenty,
      Not waste the shot.

He *like it very well,* he say—the torture.
      He say he *find it*
As sweet as do the Englishmen their sugar.
      We break his legs
For that, and he sit down and then we
      Knock his brains out.
We hear the soldiers whisper close together,
      Salvages, barbarians. . . .
These same that like to watch, for none there was
      Did try to stop it.

Monoco: One-Eyed John

You hear much of me in Nipmuck country,
  Monoco,
The Sagamore of Nashaway some call
  One-Eyed John.
How you think I lose that eye I tell you:
  Mohawk arrow.
Mohawks come, kill, steal corn, burn wetus,
  Monoco not run,
Not hide in swamp—Fight! Lose eye. Save home:
  Small thing to pay.
English worse than Mohawk: Mohawk come,
  Do mischief, go 'way.
English come, see good land, English stay and
  Spread all over
Quabaug, Quinsigamond, Squinshepauke,
  Weshakim. . . .
Build homes, have many children, want more land,
  Push out Indians.
We find out what secret English plan is:
  Put all Indians
In Praying Towns, no more go here, there . . .
  Put up wetu,
Take down wetu, move free across land
  Like sun in heaven.

Nipmuck people long time friends with Metacom;
  His old father,
Massasoit, spend much time at Quabaug
  Here with us.
Now Philip come and wake us up to fight
  These Englishmen.

Wabaquasset, Quabaug, Nipmuck, Nashaway;
      Pocumtuck,
Squakeag, Norwottuck, Agawam, from
      Both sides of river,
Meet with him in council, hear him speak
      Much truth of heart:
This be our last chance to live with honor
      As free people.
The old men no want war, so much afraid of
      English power.
But young men say: *Why shall we have peace*
      To be made slaves,
And either be killed or sent away to sea
      To Barbadoes. . . . Let us
Live as long as we can and die like men . . .
      Not be enslaved.
When each man speak his piece and my turn come,
      I say—"No more talk!
I join my brother Philip now in war
      Against the English."
Then all together gathered chant as one:
      "It is well! It is well!"
Matoonas, Muttaump, Netus, Shoshanim:
      Sagamore Sam. . . .
All pledge faith to Philip. Quaqunquaset:
      Sagamore John,
Much eager then to go fight English, but
      So quick change friends
When all goes wrong and Indians not win.
      That viper snake
To save his skin betrays our friend, Matoonas.
      He ties him up,
Takes him to the English, asking please that
      He may kill him

By his own hand, to show he much repent
    He warred on them.
Young Peter Jethro, Old Jethro's son,
    That Praying Indian,
So much Christian Bible in him, he turns
    His own father in.
We see in the end who is loathsome louse,
    And who a man.

When blood up passion-hot at council dance,
    None afraid then.
Sagamore, sachem, warrior, *pniese*. . .
    All bravest men
So eager we show the English this time
    They not stop us.
Then who show up at Mt. Wachusett
    But my old friend,
James Quannapohit (almost worse than
    Sagamore John).
With him Christian Indian, Job Kattenanit,
    Who tell how they
Escape from off Deer Island out in harbor,
    Where English now
Send Praying Indians, with no food, no blanket,
    No shelter for winter.
They no care about poor Indians—say:
    Let 'em die out there.
These two say they run away here. Old friend
    Quannapohit,
I believe him, think him good man, when together
    We fought Mohawks.
Some say they be spies and we should kill them.
    I say, *I will kill*

Whomsoever shall kill Quannapohit.
     When I find out
Those men were sent out here to spy on us,
     It stabs my heart.

Matoonas, first with mischief, burns the town
     Of Mendon down.
Muttaump, smart and fierce as cougar, sinks claws
     In Brookfield next.
English puzzle why we do this, why we
     Join with Philip,
When they so good to us, make us all these
     Praying Towns:
Wamesit, Natick, Hassanamesit. . . .
     Make us all good
Christian Indians—that pray, not think—
     Not think, not know
Their plan for Indian is—kill his soul;
     Kill his soul and
Take his land, make him live by English law,
     No more Indian way.
Worse than killing Indian is—kill his soul,
     Make it so small
Maybe it disappear down hole in ground.
     Indian soul . . .
That friends the grass, tree, river, blue-thatch sky,
     Whose cloud flowers
Send the thirsting Earth her rain to fill the streams
     And green the corn.
Indian's soul is spirit garment spread
     North, East, South, West.
It calls the bear, the deer, Good animals,
     Come give us meat.

And brings in time the full Fish Moon to send
    The shad and salmon
Swimming fat and thick into our nets.
    Indian's soul . . . it
Sends the dream that speaks our life path to us,
    And teaches us
The spirit song we keep inside our heart
    To sing at death.
I ask the Englishmen, can Christian god
    Do that for us?

Deerfield, Northfield, Springfield, Hatfield—
    Strike here, there—
Medfield, Framingham, Lancaster—where we
    Take hostages;
And preacher wife Mary Rowlandson, she
    Be one of them.
So to make the English crazy, I start
    A little story.
First I tell some Indians, who tell to
    Other Indians,
Who tell some Englishmen, who send it on
    Down to the ears
Of Reverend Rowlandson: no need now for
    Ransom money,
His wife decide she marry One-Eyed John—
    We have our fun!

I tell my men when we make raid on Groton,
    Burn houses, barns . . .
Everything but Captain Parker's garrison,
    And one close next,
Where I go have good talk with him; tell him,
    "Parker, listen,

We good neighbors now, so I be your friend."
    Say, "Pay attention,
You get good sermon why we fight this war,
    Learn why Indians
So long angry they flare up so soon as
    Philip light the spark."
Tell him, if he listen I can teach him much;
    Talk all night at him.
Tell him, too bad we burn his meetinghouse,
    Maybe Sunday
He come fish with me. —No place left to pray.
    Tell him, when we
Burn Medfield we leave behind this note
    James-the-Printer wrote,
In his good Harvard College English, which
    I recite for him:
Know by this paper, that the Indians
    Thou hast
Provoked to wrath and anger, will war
    This 21 years
If you will. There are many Indians yet.
    We come 300
At this time. You must consider
    The Indians lose
Nothing but their life. You must lose your fair
    Houses and cattle.

Captain Parker wants to know when I be through
    Haranguing him.
I tell him, "You not much social, Captain."
    I ask him is he
Friend of Captain Moseley, and what he
    Think of him?

What he think of that kind of Christian man
    Who sets dogs on
To tear to pieces poor old Indian woman
    Who not hurt him?
Ask him, how come it not be such bad thing
    When Englishmen
Do torture? But, oh! when Indian . . . then
    Him savage beast.
I tell him he so lucky we good neighbors,
    What happen to
Those captains, Beers, Lathrop, Hutchinson,
    Not come to him—
No sir! My good old neighbor, I look out for.
    Then I ask him,
Does he know what good work Indians do
    At Deerfield?
Tell him, men who stop from crossing brook
    To gather grapes
Have big surprise to find the trees so full
    Of juicy bullets.
When we see Moseley and his pirate men,
    We call out
Taunting him: *Come, Moseley, come,*
    You seek Indians,
You want Indians; here is Indians
    Enough for you.
We kill there so many, English name it
    Bloody Brook.

Muttaump, Monoco, Shoshanim, we show 'em,
    You build, we burn:
Marlborough, Sudbury, Weymouth, Simsbury. . . .
    I say, "Parker,

Captain, my good neighbor, we just begin:
    Chelmsford, Concord,
Watertown, Cambridge, Roxbury, Boston . . .
    They be next."
And in my "Harvard College" English, tell him,
    What me will, me do.

Sagamore John

Horowannit, Abigganosh, Quaqunquaset:
  So many names,
And each one marks another crossing on
  The life path.
For this, my story, you need only one: John,
  Sagamore John
Of Pakachoog, the Christian village near
  Qinsigamond,
In Nipmuck country, where I was leader,
  Well regarded.
There, as constable, Matoonas also
  Served with me;
Friend of better days, before the war, before
  Our falling out.
Together we kept order and followed
  English law,
Its Christian principles, so said were for
  The good of all.
And then one day John Eliot comes with
  Daniel Gookin
To see if preacher they have sent us shows
  Much progress in
His work of making Christians, turning us
  From our old ways,
Old "heathen" ways—the ancient ways—
  Civilizing us.

But there is other purpose brings them here
  To us this day,
This heavy thing they must needs say, and we—
  And we must needs

Understand: no Indian shall own his land
    Unless the court
Grant him the right to it. And one thing more . . .
    The court does not
Grant land to Indians who live outside of
    Praying Towns.
So now we see what is the government plan:
    Make all Christian
And put 'em in a pen; like keeping hogs,
    Not for free men.
No more come and go on open land
    For Indian?
How could this be? I would not believe it,
    This strange thing,
From any man's mouth but them, Eliot
    And Gookin—
Who tell me, since 1644 *this* has been the law:
    When Great Sachems
Cutshamekin, Mascononomo, Chickatabut,
    By some treaty
Submit themselves, their subjects and their lands
    Under the government
And jurisdiction of the Massachusetts
    To be governed
And protected by them according to their
    Just law. . . .
"Just" law? Not this—a trap, a snare is what
    They tell me of—
To take by craft, by stealth, the tribal lands.
    No sachem,
No Indian, no one of sense would sign
    This thing, this treaty,
If he in honest truth knew what it was
    That he so did.

Who but great fool would give our lands away
　　　To English rule?—
The tribal lands, these lands from all of time
　　　Our people's home—
No more to have and leave them for our children?
　　　Never! Never would he!
When I finish with my angry outburst,
　　　Eliot and Gookin
Will not look at me, not let me catch their eye;
　　　They look away.
All they have to say is . . . it is for our *good*.
　　　And—it's the law.

When Philip comes, there are many eager
　　　Now to join him.
Nipmucks, Nashaways, Quabaugs—and I was one.
　　　Not all that pray
Are Christian, some down under his skin
　　　Is still Indian.
I go on raids with them, Matoonas, Muttaump,
　　　Monoco, and
Shoshanim, burning towns, killing cattle
　　　And Englishmen.
But war drags on and by the time of snows,
　　　Each day we weaken;
Lose many men, people sick, villages,
　　　Cornfields burnt.
More than Praying Indians and Mohegans,
　　　It was hunger—
The strongest ally of the English—hunger
　　　That would crush us.
And when they capture Muttaump's wife
　　　And Shoshanim's,

We meet in council and I say, let us make
      What peace we can.
We owe no more to Philip, and this war
      Cannot be won.
Let us begin the ransom talks for
      Mary Rowlandson.
Then Shoshanim agrees to send a letter
      Down to Boston.

When all the English captives are returned,
      I go myself
With enemy scalp and flag of truce
      To make my peace,
And say I am much sorry that I fight them,
      That Philip forced me.
I say I will come back with Nipmucks ready
      To surrender.
But then Matoonas . . . *his heart so big hot*
      Within him,
Will not go along; they hanged his oldest son—
      He hates the English.
He shows me scorn, says I am a woman—
      Not a warrior.
I knock him down and tie him up, and then
      His other son;
Take both of them as prisoner to Boston.
      And yes, I ask
That I may shoot him, to show the English
      I do repent my
Wickedness and beg of them forgiveness
      For those wrongs done.

If all the gods, Indian and English, knew
      How sore my heart,

That I should live to do this thing, betray
     My friend Matoonas,
They would forgive and end the punishment
     I now must live:
A man made powerless, placed under Captain
     Thomas Prentice
By order of the court; my lands all gone
     To Englishmen—
Daniel Gookin with the rest of them
     That would have me
From my home, and take possession of
     Quinsigamond.
These are the "just rights" given Indians—
     "For our own good."
I cannot live this way; my people with me,
     We are ready—
Some night soon, quietly we slip away
     To Canada country.

Shoshanim: Sagamore Sam

Yes, I do blame Philip now for putting me
    In this bad place,
For the trouble he has brought upon
    The Nashaway.
Troubles, in truth, begin when Christians come:
    Eliot and Gookin,
Who think to make us live like Englishmen,
    In Praying Towns.
John Eliot, when Sholan dies, thinks *he*
    Knows what is best
To pick for us who should be sagamore
    Of Nashaway,
When Shoshanim—I was him most ready
    To be sachem.
But Eliot wants Sholan's nephew: Matthew,
    A *Christian* Indian.
And put his big-buckle foot in where he
    Had no business,
Spreading stories I am that bad kind
    That takes strong drink.
How much you think he like it I should come
    And pick for him
His governor in Boston there to make
    His laws for him?
When Matthew dies and I am sachem then,
    First thing I say:
Please, Englishmen, I thank you not to sell
    My people rum.

Why did I send to Boston humble letters
    Begging peace

Of them I swore must first beg peace of me?
    Before I tell you,
You go back, remember how I answer
    First time letter come
To learn our mind, see if maybe we make
    Peace with them:
We now give answer by this one man,
    But if you like
My answer send one more . . . with all true heart
    And with all your mind . . .
Because you know and we know your heart
    Great sorrowful
With crying for your lost many many hundred
    Men and all your
House and all your land, and women, child
    And cattle,
As all your thing that you have lost and on
    Your backside stand.

One reason only why we change our tone,
    Later begging peace,
More than my pride I must protect my wife
    And children
Taken prisoner from Weshakim, and
    Muttaump's wife
Is one of these. And he and all of us
    With families,
In such danger maybe to be sent away
    On ships for slaves,
Were ready then to do . . . say . . . try anything
    That we could think.
Even plead with them in Jesus name,
    So desperate now

Were we become in our distress we have
        One thought alone,
To make our letter strong in words that most
        Will move their heart.
For many times John Eliot has said
        It is the law,
As written in the Bible, Christian men
        Must all forgive
And turn unto their enemies with love.
        —We see if this be so.

I do not think a man like Captain Moseley
        Much ready to
Forgive and love—not him! There is one who
        Hates all Indians!
In Quabaug fight we laugh so hard that time
        To see him snatch
His periwig from off his head and tuck it
        In his britches:
Umh, Umh, me no stay here fight Engishmon,
        Engishmon
Got two head. Engishmon got two head.
        Me cut off un,
He got noder beder un he put on.
        And even now,
When there is little left to draw a smile,
        I think of it and laugh.

It sorrowed us to learn that Captain Tom
        Was hanged,
Wattasacompanum, Nipmuck Sachem.
        For he was one
That never wished to leave his Praying Town
        And fight the English;

We tell him, you best come along with us
      To Menemesit.
If Eliot himself has tried and failed
      To save the Sachem,
What might any one of us expect from
      English justice?
We so ready now to think what can we do
      To end this war,
Sagamore John goes down to Boston under
      Flag of truce
To ask what terms the English want if they
      Would make the peace,
And gives his word to set all captives free.
      Then one—two—days,
Back he goes, this time with "enemy" scalp
      To show some proof
How we are done with Philip now, so they
      Will better trust us.
He tells them I will come next time with him
      To do surrender.
But John goes back alone. —No, not alone,
      But not with me!
Hundred-sixty Indians surrender
      With him. —And two
He brings—that were his friends—all tied
      And stoutly bound,
Matoonas and his son; he hands them to
      The English.
In this we learn what kind of man is John
      Of Pakachoog,
Who lies and say he never wished to join
      With Philip,
That Philip came and made to him a threat
      If he would not.

How could this be? —For Philip was not yet
    At Menemesit
When Captain Hutchinson is shot from where
    We lay in ambush.
I saw it all: John is first to fire and I see
    Hutchinson fall.

Muttaump, Monoco, Shoshanim—always
    Best true friends,
Maybe we go north together now to
    Wannalancet.
The Pennacook have been at peace, maybe
    We mix in with them.

When I stand still, look all around here,
    Look up, look down
Wachusett, see all this place, this woods,
    This grass, this trees. . . .
Think how this always been here Indian's home,
    Then English come, say
Be Indian's friend, then tell him how everything
    All wrong with him:
Wrong house, wrong clothes, wrong dance,
    Wrong speak words,
Wrong bad gods. Call him savage, must show him
    Better how to live.
No, not better how to live— Better how to die—
    Like sick animal
When the wolves are after him and he run, run, run
    Till they catch him.

Wannalancet

As he prepared for his long journey to
    The spirit land,
The season of his days nearing its end,
    Passaconaway,
My father, Great Sachem of the Pennacook,
    Distinguished powwaw,
Called us, his children, to him one last time
    That we might know
The judgment of his great and powerful mind,
    Whose sacred gifts
The Master Of All Life bestowed on him:
    Interpreter
Of signs and portents, dreams and visions.
    And as he wished
To leave with us his foresight, in his wisdom
    He counseled thus:

I am now going the way of all flesh,
    Or ready to die,
And not likely to see you meet together
    Any more.
I will now leave this word of counsel with you,
    That you may heed
How you quarrel with the English, for though
    You may do them
Much mischief, yet assuredly you will all
    Be destroyed,
And rooted off the earth if you so do; for,
    I was as much
An enemy to the English, at their first coming
    Into these parts,

As anyone whatsoever, and did try all ways
    And possible means
To have destroyed them, at least to have
    Prevented them
Settling down here, but I could in no way
    Effect it; therefore,
I advise you never to contend with the English
    Or make war with them.

And thus have I, Wannalancet, elder son
    And sachem,
Carrying the burden of wise leadership
    For the people of
The Merrimack, paid solemn heed to my
    Good father's words,
And in all ways avoided any conflict
    With the English,
Though many times provoked beyond the edge
    Of patience
With their appetite for more, and always more,
    Of Indian land.

We see our woodlands melt before our eyes
    Like snows of spring.
They have plowed and planted my own ground
    As if it were
Their right to do, while I despair of space
    For my own corn.
We see their numbers wax and multiply
    While Indians
Grow few and fewer, stricken by each plague,
    By pox and flux,
Such evils we knew nothing of before
    The English came.

Never to contend with them—my father
    So enjoined. . . .
How often have I swallowed down the words
    The good man spoke,
When so consumed by wrath I felt the blood
    Pound in my head,
My very fingers flex of their own will, as if
    They felt the gun,
The club, the tomahawk within their grasp;
    But steadfast kept
To Passaconaway's admonishment,
    Even when provoked
By Captain Moseley's vicious raid upon
    Our peaceful village.
What had Wannalancet done but move
    Our people north,
Declaring our neutrality, our wish
    To live in peace,
Removed from all the warring tribes within
    These territories?
The very act of our removal was,
    In that dark mind
Of Moseley, judged a sign of Pennacook
    Hostility.
He burnt our village in pure malice as
    A warning to us.
Nor did I let my warriors strike him back,
    But led my people
Ever deeper into the forest fastness
    Farther north.

And when the roiling torrent of rebellion
    That swept up

Nipmuck patriots, turned and left them stranded,
    Great numbers
Of the vanquished in desperation fled
    To us for refuge.
Promises of amnesty for Indians
    That shed no blood
Gave little comfort to the leaders,
    Who might expect
No more of mercy than the hangman's rope
    Would give them.
Thus Muttaump, Monoco, Shoshanim. . . .
    Were now my guests
Despite the treaty I had signed allowing
    None a refuge.
Yet when a man within your sight is drowning,
    Will you not
With little thought put forth the hand of rescue?
    And would he not
In panicked desperation seize even
    At the eelgrass
Though it break off in his hand and float on
    With the current?

So it was with these in my protection,
    Whom Peter Jethro
And his Praying Indian friends, by accident
    —Or design—
Lured here to "treat of peace," or so they thought,
    With Major Waldron.
Thus his father, Old Jethro (Tantamous),
    And all the rest
Fell fast into a clever trap the wily
    Major set,

A stratagem to capture them at no
    Risk to his men.
When told it was a "training exercise,"
    And so taken in,
The warriors discharged their weapons
    Harmlessly in air,
Whereupon the Major's men surrounded
    And disarmed them.
The warriors that came to Cocheco
    To talk of peace
Were shipped on down to Boston: an ignoble
    Breach of trust.
Waldron's ears were closed to supplication,
    I could not save
These wretched souls whose fate had left my hands.
    No, there would be
No mercy for the warrior sagamores,
    Nor for their families—
A tragic end: Muttaump, Monoco, Old Jethro,
    Shoshanim . . .
Each, on Boston Common would meet, in turn,
    The hanging tree.

O wise counselor of men, my father,
    Who cautioned,
Never contend with the English, nor
    Make war with them.
Yet it matters less and less who did and
    Who did not resist,
Either way our fate comes to the same:
    Indians' lands,
Ancestral lands, are lost to all alike;
    I fear the worst.

If we remain what future is there here
       But grief for us?
I shall lead my people north to Canada . . .
       Among the French.

Quinnapin

Quinnapin and Canonchet, cousins close
　　　　As brothers,
Together we grew up, great nephews of
　　　　Canonicus:
Chief Narragansett Sachem, rich in years
　　　　And wisdom.
From him we learned the lore and history
　　　　Of our people,
What high place we held, the many tribes that
　　　　Paid us tribute;
The rivalries, the enemies, the friends. . . .
　　　　My cousin's wetu,
Where Aunt Wawalom fixed my favorite treats,
　　　　Was second home;
To Uncle Miantonomo I was so much
　　　　Another son.
And when we came of age and it was time
　　　　To take our place
Beside the council fire, though known to be
　　　　More playful
Than my cousin Canonchet, I was no less
　　　　The warrior.
And none there was would find me wanting when
　　　　The time should come.

And come it did at Great Swamp Fort, where
　　　　Second-in-command
To Canonchet, I fought the soldiers
　　　　Hand to hand
When we ran out of powder for the guns,
　　　　That day the English

Came with single purpose—kill us, kill us all,
    Firing the wetus:
The aged, the sick, the young and helpless. . . .
    The English, merciless.

It was but days before that Metacom
    Had come and gone,
Both thanking Canonchet for sheltering
    His people,
And pressing him to get our Narragansetts
    In the field.
We hoped to put him off until the spring's
    Green leafing out
Would give us better cover, but the attack
    Upon the fort
Had changed all that, and we were in it now:
    We would strike back!
Philip went to Schaghticoke intent to
    Purchase weapons
From the French, the Dutch, and meet with tribes
    Around those parts.
His big mistake was thinking he could talk
    The Mohawks into
Giving some support, and nearly lost his scalp
    For all his trouble.

So many years we fought the Wampanoags,
    Now here we were,
Two bears in one same den and learning
    How to get along.
And there was one I am, oh, so much pleased
    To welcome to
The Narragansett den: Queen Weetamoo,
    Pocasset Sachem.

I look at her look at me and think . . . *humm,*
      Wife number three?
The comely queen reminds me she has had
      Four husbands
Of her station and, *saunks* in her own right,
      She has no need
To join the two I have to pleasure me.
      To her I say,
"You have your husbands one then the other,
      I have my wives
Same time together—each wife in separate wetu:
      We make do."
I wink and wait and, yes, at last she laughs
      And takes my hand.

I think the spirits like to use us for some
      Game they play:
Send joy, send trouble, and watch the people
      How they handle.
We buried our dead from the Great Swamp Fort
      And settled
The old and wounded with those who offered
      To care for them.
The rest of us would go with Canonchet
      To Mt. Wachusett
And join the band of patriot Indians there.
      We met at first
A hostile welcome, shot at by these Nipmucks
      Who want some proof
The Narragansetts come as friends to them.
      But when we show
Some enemy scalps, well then they see what
      Side we fight on

And cheer so loud I think they hear it
      All the way to Boston.

We came a storm in numbers strong and
      Fell on Lancaster,
And left them many dead to count;
      Exultant warriors
Scoffing, jeering what good turn we do these
      Lucky Christians—
To send them to heaven so soon.
      Mock them? Yes.
At Sudbury, I hear a Nipmuck "pray"
      Above his victim,
Come Lord Jesus, if thou canst, save this poor
      Englishman,
Whom I am now about to kill. —Why does
      He show such scorn?
Maybe so angry Englishmen scorn him
      That keeps the gods
Of his own worship, and call him "heathen."
      —And maybe angry
They take his land, no place left to live
      But Praying Town.
Sometimes so crazy angry in your pain,
      You mock, you—torture!
You don't think Englishmen do this? Then you
      Don't pay attention.
We took, for ransom, captives in the raid
      At Lancaster.
Mary Rowlandson I bought from him
      That captured her,
To work as servant maid for Weetamoo.
      That preacher wife,

I tell you, she was not an easy one:
    Two proud women
I must get between from time to time to
    Save her from a beating.

The news came like the lightning flash that splits
    Apart the sky:
Canonchet was dead! —My cousin, our captain!
    They said he
Would not bargain for his life: a noble death
    Delivered by
Base hands, Oweneco, that Mohegan—
    English Indian!
We vowed never to surrender, we would
    Fight on to the end.
And thus it was for him, and shall be so
    For me ere long,
If I read well the powwaws—what they see,
    But do not say.

So many of us gathered in one place
    And food so scarce,
And planting time so near, and nothing but
    This bitter war.
More and more the Nipmuck sachems grumble:
    Why they ever
Let that Pokanoket get them into this?
    And how can each
Now make his separate peace and maybe even
    Save his neck.
No longer welcome here, or even safe,
    We finish up
The ransom business, and with our people
    Leave Wachusett.

The day is spent preparing for the dance—
        Dance that takes us
To the spirit world, as in all things we
        Seek their favor.
Weetamoo and I will lead the dance, as
        Worthy of our station.
She, bejeweled, in kersey coat, red stockings
        And white slippers;
And I, in Holland shirt sewn up with lace
        And silver buttons,
My stockings held by garters tricked out with
        Dangling shillings.
We made a handsome pair, engirdled round
        With precious wampum,
Which as we danced we cast away to all
        Those gathered there.

The sagamores agree to twenty pounds,
        Some seed corn and
Tobacco, to give up Mary Rowlandson.
        But sick at heart
His Nipmuck friends would turn on him like this,
        Philip takes no part.
As she was my captive, I have final say,
        And I tell him,
Mr. Hoar, the messenger from Boston,
        "Just one thing more:
Bring me first a pint of liquor and then
        I let her go."

I get a little drunk and act the fool,
        I later hear
From Weetamoo, who tells me how I am
        One minute

Toasting Mr. Hoar and his good health,
    And in the next,
I am a raving crazy man who wants to
    Hang him for a rogue!
I get sober soon enough when we leave
    Behind Wachusett,
Carrying such loss with us, the splintering
    Of our people,
Death of the confederacy: this that was
    Our one best chance.

Weetamoo

I have as well been known as Namumpum,
      Tatapanum,
But you will now remember me as she
      Who ruled her people,
The Pocassets, proudly as Squaw Sachem,
      Queen Weetamoo;
Sister of Wootonekanuske, King Philip's wife.
      We married kings,
We two, the sons of Ousamequin:
      Massasoit.
Who, had he lived beyond the years allowed,
      Would curse the day
He looked upon an Englishman with aught
      But hate in heart.
Oh, had he known the fate in store for these
      His sons! That this—
This Winslow—spawn of him whose band he saved
      From certain death,
Would turn upon his Indian hosts within
      A generation;
And Alexander's death would follow soon
      Upon his own,
For having proved too sharp a thorn lodged in
      The English foot,
Which trespassed and then trampled all that stood
      Against it.

With no just cause did he, Josiah Winslow,
      Brandishing a gun,
Break in upon us at our hunting lodge beside
      Monponsett Pond,

Where we were gathered at the morning meal,
    Demanding Alexander,
On some false charge, go with him to Plymouth;
    That to resist
Would be his death. Complying, so it was!
    Thence he, who had
Been strong and well, grew of a sudden ill.
    Oh, I was there
When they sent for the medicine doctor
    To administer
The physic that before another sun
    Would kill—not heal!
And having no remorse, they said it was
    The Sachem's wrath
At being summoned that roiled in him and
    Caused his death.
Evil men, they poison him, and then they
    Blame their victim!

It is that devil book that makes them crazy;
    It's full of spells.
They use these on our Indians—like
    Sassamon—
To make them leave our people and join with
    Praying clans.
John Eliot sends them preaching to us, buzzing
    Like mosquitoes.
Corbitant, my father, knew the English;
    He could see what
Massasoit, in all his wisdom, had chosen
    Not to own:
That we were raising up a nest of vipers
    In our midst.

Many times he said it: "Trust not the Whites!
    The French, the Dutch
Are bad enough, but English are the worst
    Of all that come,
Hungry for our land to plow and farm,
    Cut down the trees
And leave no place for Indian to hunt, or
    Animal to live."
"Do not be fooled," he said. "They take and take,
    They do not give."

They seemed as gods when first he looked on them,
    The goods they owned:
Tools, guns, the coats of wool and cotton cloth;
    No Indian
Had ever seen such truck before they came.
    My father warned
I should not love their pretty things too much.
    Little heed I paid,
My passion to look beautiful was strong.
    I wanted them,
The stockings knit of cotton, red and white,
    The necklaces,
Ropes of beads and coins to drape and dress.
    I reasoned thus,
As Queen of the Pocassets, should I
    Not look the part?
For was it not *my* foot that led the dance?
    I was vain, yes.
And now it all seems as a dream—the clothes,
    My pretty clothes
Soiled, torn— Look at me now, a queen in rags;
    And my husband

In their hands and good as dead.—O Quinnapin,
    Must each die alone?
You have proved the better man to me,
    To Philip and
The cause, than many others he had reason
    To put trust in.

Awashonks, no more constant than a feather
    In the wind,
Has made a desperate deal to save herself,
    Surrendering now
Her warriors to fight with Captain Church—
    With him—against us;
Against Pocasset, Pokanoket—brothers
    To Sakonnet.
Might I have done the same? But at what price?
    —Betray Metacom,
My kin . . . the ancient fathers . . . and the voice
    That speaks within?
He said it broke his heart that she would turn
    Her back on him.

The truth is . . . oh, I too did hesitate,
    Then Philip came
Reminding me of who I was, by birth,
    By marriage and,
Yes, by the sacred honor of our race.
    And it was then
I knew I could no longer live as wife
    To Petananuet,
So willing had he been to cast his lot
    With Englishmen.
We parted ways, and thus I followed on
    With Philip.

Our hopes were high and fed on desperation
  To be free . . . or die.
His wish had been to wait and gather in
  The nations,
But when they hanged his men . . . for Sassamon,
  It forced his hand.

Still, there were victories to cheer before
  The losses came.
It might have even gone our way had but
  The Narragansetts
Joined us at the start, while they temporized
  Much time was lost.
But Philip showed withal a cool restraint,
  A thoughtfulness.
The man did even show much kindness
  To our captives—
To Mary Rowlandson—whose face I slapped,
  And once did
Threaten with a stick, when she refused
  To tear a scrap
From off her apron, needed for a newborn's
  Swaddling cloth.
My own papoose had died but days before;
  Oh, I was wroth!
With food so scarce and precious, Philip fed
  The English woman,
And gave her comfort with the promise
  Of a ransom.
Yet there was in him never once the thought
  Of giving up.
When left and right the faint of heart deserted,
  He fought on

As if the warriors that did remain were
  Each a thousand men.
And like the whipped-up waves within a storm,
  His energy
Did drive us on until the last faint hope
  Was snuffed.

I have not strength, nor spark of life in me,
  Nor wish for aught
But rest: let it end now, here where I am.
  Let it be done!
The sticks of my poor raft break up, drift off,
  Oh, let me drown!
I have no wish to swim, to struggle on.
  Great river, Titicut,
Take my tears and wash all sorrow from them,
  Take my breath
And give it to the trees that stand with arms
  Upraised in waiting,
Take my spirit and carry it to that
  Good land beyond.
And when they come with barking dogs and guns
  To take me in . . .
When they find Weetamoo she'll be at rest
  In your soft womb.
The waters, sun-warmed, open to me like
  My mother's arms,
When she would lift and comfort me from some
  Small childhood hurt.
O Titicut, you have ever been to us
  The truest friend,
Who gave us fish and brought the water birds,
  Carried our canoes

From place to place; times we danced and feasted
      Here along the shore,
Built our fires and watched the moon watch us
      Till it grew white.
O moon, O sun, will you remember us:
      The People of First Light?

Annawon

Through the shadowed wood you hear it echo:
    Iootash! Iootash!
Oh, it is there on the wind if you listen:
    Iootash! Iootash!
The whispering leaves do not forget the cry
    Of Annawon,
Rallying the men to *stand and fight!* Fight on:
    Iootash!
Ah, but the bullet found the Sachem's heart,
    And Captain Church
At last had got his quarry—the powwaw's
    Prophesy fulfilled—
No Englishman would kill the Sachem;
    It was Alderman,
An Indian, the traitor with the gun
    That took him down.

So sorrowful an end to Philip's reign—
    Massasoit's line. . . .
The sun has traveled many times around
    The great sky path
Since Annawon and Massasoit were young:
    Proud, lusty men!
I served him all his days, his chief war captain;
    And then his sons,
Each in turn as called upon, the ties were strong.
    With the signing
Of the Taunton Treaty I saw war grow
    In Philip's heart—
Times he would stop, look up as if the sky
    Were listening,

90

And like a bite of something bitter, spit out
    The galling words:
"Naughtiness of my heart"! War roiled in him,
    And on the tongues
Of the murmuring young, eager to begin
    Without a plan.
We do not pick the fruit before the fruit is ripe,
    I cautioned them.
But their ears were stuffed with moss, they struck
    The hornets' nest
At Swansea: the deed was done, the war begun,
    The timing wrong.

We fled from Pokanoket to Pocasset,
    To Nipsachuck;
Each time escaping, but with losses we
    Could not make up.
Mohegans and English, two breaths behind,
    Dogging our steps,
Our fate in the juggling hands of the gods.
    With less than
Forty able fighting men—women, children
    And wounded
Traveling with us—we made it to Asquash,
    To our allies
The Nipmucks. And when at Menemesit
    Philip learns of
The attack on Brookfield, Muttaump's strong and
    Able leadership,
The work of Monoco and Sagamore John,
    He gives to each
Much precious wampum unstrung from his coat,
    For brave deeds done.

The darkest days would come at Schaghticoke,
    When having won
The River Tribes, Mahicans, and Pocumtucks
    Over to us,
To our regret we seek out Mohawks next.
    All their fearsome
Strength and fury they turn on us instead,
    Massacring many.
Do not believe the rumor Philip hatched
    A foiled plan
To kill "a scattering of them"—and put it
    On the English—
Stirring them up to strike back in revenge.
    Let truth be known:
There never was such plan! It was instead
    The New York governor,
Fearing war would spread into his country,
    Who turned them loose
To drive us out of Schaghticoke; and thus
    We lost at once,
Our warriors, our allies, and it seemed
    Perhaps the war.

Weakened, we return to Nipmuck country,
    Philip carrying
The burden of our losses as a stone
    Upon his heart.
So much not going well, would soon get worse,
    Much worse, Canonchet . . .
Canonchet is killed; the news comes hard,
    Freezing the blood.
Philip spoke no word, swallowing pain and rage,
    He clutched his breast

As if to keep his heart within its cage.
      Canonchet was dead!
Quinnapin, Pessacus, Pomham, Potok—
      All good men—
But Canonchet . . . Canonchet was dead. No one
      Could replace him!

Alliances were breaking up, Nipmucks
      Losing heart.
Sickness, hunger, the need to keep moving
      Whole families . . .
More real, more painful now than all the fear
      Of English justice.
Talk has turned to ransoming the captives,
      How much to ask?
This, though we had driven them from Brookfield,
      Deerfield, Lancaster . . .
Were pushing them back, back, back to the coast.
      Then—just then—does
The fire in the heart go out, and the hand
      With success
In its grasp lets it drop, after Sudbury,
      In the English lap.

When Philip learns the Nipmuck sachems go
      Behind his back
To treat of peace in secret talks with Boston—
      The broken trust—
It so darkens his thoughts, I watch him
      Like a troubled father,
Much grieved to see him turning inward,
      Brooding solitary,
Suffering abandonment by those he
      Counted on

To stand with him unwavering to the end.
    This peace would be
A coward's peace, a soiled garment he
    Disdains to touch.
It is time to leave Wachusett and return
    To Pokanoket.
There, fight on—fight on alone if we must.
    Iootash!

As warming spring calls fish to come and spawn,
    It called from hunger
Indians to feast on them. We made our camp
    At Peskeompscut,
There beside the falls on the shores of the
    Connecticut,
To rest, repair our guns, and lay our plans
    For going home.
If we wanted English beef, we raided
    Hatfield farms.
But are not long in this good place before
    Our camp is found.
Those who in careless ease relaxed their guard
    Are shot in
Their beds where they lay, while those escaping
    To the river
Are swept along the cataract and dashed
    Upon the rapids.
Great numbers die this way, but we regroup
    And stage a rout.
And Captain Turner, who led his men in, does
    Not lead them out.
We bury our dead and make our way home,
    Where the enemy,

94

Like ants upon a hill, swarm all around.
      We may not rest
Two nights in any one same place, but jump
      Like nervous hares,
From bush to bush, den to den, scampering
      Among the swamps,
Striking where we can. And running, running,
      Running out of time.

The moon was strong and full, the Harvest Moon,
      Over Squannakonk
The night Church found my camp, this harvester
      Of men, who gathers
Indians to fight for him by force of charm—
      Or fear of slave ships.
Yet I could show respect to him, a man
      Of proven mettle.
Descending the slope of my encampment,
      He took a chance
That faithless luck, deserting Annawon,
      Would fly to him.
Thus we meet face to face at last—too late
      For *Iootash!*
Church has taken all my weapons; we meet
      As two proud men
Who take the measure of each other, and when
      I speak at last
To him in his own tongue, it makes no small
      Impression.

This Benjamin Church is not the worst of
      Englishmen.
I would not be bested by a lesser man,
      A Talcott or a Moseley.

He came, he said, to sit and sup with me,
      Preferring
Cow to horse, as though he were my guest
      And not my captor.
Deep into the night we talk, sharing tales
      Like old companions.
I could surrender to this man, with honor,
      The sovereign regalia
Of my Sachem, whom I served with honor:
      The war had died with him.

Wootonekanuske

Great Spirit, giver of life, father of all
    That has been,
All that is to come, you know our paths,
    Our traveled ways.
You count the tribes from your high lodge,
    Number our days.
You set in place the sun, the moon, and all
    The little lights.
You make the trees to branch above our heads,
    The corn to grow,
The creatures of the wood and of the sea
    To thrive and give
The goodness of their meat that we might live.
    O Great Spirit,
You who dwell in mystery, hear your daughter,
    Wootonekanuske.
They have slain my husband, Metacom,
    Our cause undone.
They have taken his head from his body,
    That his spirit,
Cowwewonck, may not find its way along
    The path to you.
O ever blessed manitto, *Kautantowwit*,
    Lead his spirit,
His noble spirit, I pray you, to your house
    Of peace and good.

Good spirits, be with us in our sorrow:
    Shelter my son,
He, from toe to brow, his father's son.
    A sachem's heart

Beats in his breast. The blood of Metacom,
     Of Massasoit,
Of all the noble Wampanoag line
     Lives on in him.
I seldom call my boy by his man's name,
     I call him, Love.
Although at his eight years, it makes him blush
     And shy away.
Keep him, Great Spirit, from the vengeance
     Of the English.
Stay their cruel and wrathful god's harsh hand,
     In whose name
They steal, they kill, they sell us off as slaves.
     Master Of Life,
You dwell in mists and yet you see what is
     And is to be,
The length of each one's life, its outer end,
     How it shall come.
I think perhaps it is a kindness much
     Is kept from us.

The soldiers brought us here to Mr. Keith,
     In this they call
The parsonage, to be his prisoners kept
     Until such time
As they have reasoned out what punishment
     They want for us.
I think this man is kind, and does not want
     To have us killed.
Those others do not have his gentle heart,
     I hear them talk.
I do not know their words, but in their voices
     Hear a darkness.

They came through exulting, the Plymouth men,
    With their trophy,
My husband's head made ghastly on a pole;
    We heard the cheers.
I placed my hands against my young son's ears,
    Who understood.
He knew his father's fate, what to expect
    Of English mercy.
They keep us here locked up in hopelessness,
    Studying in
Their Bible book how to dispose of us:
    Whether to shoot,
Or hang, or put us on a slave ship to
    Some unknown land.
I'd welcome death, to have it done, to be
    With Metacom.

The night before they found us in our camp,
    A bitter sweetness . . .
Watching father and son play at skipping stones
    Over the pond,
Each one a circle widening—as with war.
    When night came on
I saw the sky's red ochre bleed like blood
    Across the water,
And the darkness drink it up, and somewhere
    Through the mist
A whippoorwill was crying its mournful sound;
    It seemed an omen.
That night a cold dream pulled my husband upright
    Out of sleep,
Wherein he saw my father, Corbitant . . .
    His spirit hand

Held out a broken tomahawk, as if to say
      The cause was lost.
And then he saw his brother, Wamsutta,
      Standing with
His head turned, gesturing over his shoulder,
      As he would do
When they would go a-hunting, signaling
      To follow him.

How many moons have climbed the sky and down,
      I have no count.
Nor of the long walks of the sun, since we came
      To this prison.
The days pass with no meaning of their own,
      For it is all
One long night in which we wait forsaken,
      Wondering what, when?

Tuspaquin: The Black Sachem

Tuspaquin (Watuspaquin), Black Sachem.
     Following my time
Of prayer and fast, the owl, great horned bird,
     Spirit of my quest,
Descended soft as snow from the cedar tree,
     Covering my youth
With purpose, naming me, "Black Sachem."
     Pronouncing
In that moment, I should read prophetic signs,
     Know of things
Beyond the mind's own light, night wisdom
     Of dreams and visions
To which the eyes of other men are blind.
     Thus I would bear
The dual gift and burden of prophesy:
     Powwaw, priest-healer,
The Black Sachem of Assawompsett
     And Nemasket—
Warrior-counselor to Metacom, husband
     To his sister.

And as it was my wish to learn of powers
     The English god
Possessed, as claimed by Sassamon, Philip's
     Christian scribe,
I gave him of my land to settle on.
     But when the dreams,
The troubled dreams began, each a new alarm,
     I cautioned Philip,
His scribe might bear with our close watching,
     And so it proved.

His death did tie his tongue, but like a stone
    Dropped in the waters
Of Assawompsett Pond, sent out ripples
    Ever widening—
From the trial and execution of the three
    Charged with his murder—
Widening into war, surrounding us
    With all its misery.
We must abandon homes for swamps, crops still
    Ripening in the fields.
It touched the heart to see the hurt in Philip,
    Who must leave
The horse he loves, his fair black stallion,
    To some Englishman.
So soon we learn . . . the way before us shall
    Be marked with losses.

When English and Mohegans fall on us
    At Nipsachuck,
I take myself apart from all distress
    To summon forth
The guardian spirits, if in their wisdom
    They will aid us.
Thus I pray until in my mind's eye I see,
    As through a mist,
Our gathered enemies, all motionless,
    Their bodies
Flowing to the ground in roots outspread,
    Where feet should be.
Here are men become as trees so did it seem,
    Held fast in place,
An army planted where it stood, unmoving,
    Still as stone.

Then, lightly as it came, the vision passed.
      I blinked awake
And sought out Philip, saying, "It is well,
      The spirits hold our
Enemies in place; let us prepare to make
      A swift escape."
Weetamoo would take her people south and
      Lodge among
The Narragansett, while we go north to
      Carry on the fight
In common cause with Nipmuck allies, who
      Have welcomed us.

Something I would tell you— Before the war
      There came to me
A dream, a spirit voice, which spoke this riddle,
      Troubling, yet consoling:
"The blown flower's seed returns to earth to wait
      The season of rebirth.
What is shall pass, what was shall come again,
      Take heart, O Sachem."
So strange an omen, so full of portent,
      Which I understood
But ill: a thorny bush that snagged and held
      My thoughts.

With the rising of the full Blood Moon
      At summer's end,
The dream returned. I spoke of it to Philip,
      Who forbade me
To talk openly of this—that it might be
      The work of some
Bad spirit wanting to confuse, to trick us
      With its riddles.

"Let us think only of the consequence
    Of loss," he said, "of how
To bring along the River Tribes, Pocumtucks,
    And the Mohawks.
If we succeed in this—and once we have
    The Narragansetts in—
With such a force these Englishmen cannot
    Prevail against us.
Let us look to the day when Indians again
    Live free as wind."
But I have grave concerns, the haunting
    Message of the dream. . . .
Was it now too late for any other course?
    And I ask myself,
Is there in truth another way for us?
    No, I think not:
The river must follow the path the stream has
    Cut in the earth.

One by one the central tribes come in and
    We feel strong.
Matoonas, Muttaump, Monoco, Shoshanim,
    Sagamore John. . . .
We throw our force against the enemy—
    And we *were* strong.
Assaults on homes and farms spread fear and dread
    Among the English.
The scattered towns within our range grow thin
    As settlers flee
From garrison to garrison. —Ah, but our enemies
    Are quick to learn
How they might win if they can starve us to
    Submission:

Burn our fields, destroy the stores of corn, and
     Keep us on the run.
Thenceforth misfortune rules, the tide now turns,
     And by all signs
We must no more abide among the Nipmuck,
     But take the war
Back to our own home ground and fight on there
     As strength allows.

With the coming of the new Fish Moon, we
     Strike again: Rehoboth,
Dartmouth, Taunton, Plymouth, Scituate. . . .
     In scattered bands
Attacking where we can. Once, twice, and again
     To Bridgewater
We pay a call and leave our surly hosts
     The smoldering ruin.
I study close the omens and stay my hand
     When bidden,
Nor think to scorn the wisdom given in signs;
     As when I see
The bear on hind legs reared—manitto! I know
     It is a god!
Then we do not attack, we quick change plan
     And turn around.
Maybe we see a deer instead, then yes,
     We lay it on
With all our force and this time burn the village
     To the ground.
When spirit powers speak their will to us,
     We show respect.
For in the end the outcome of all things
     Belongs to them.

We ask their mercies, but whether it bode
    Good or ill
We are their agents and we do their will
    As bidden. Yes,
 Even as we are driven from our homes
    And hunted down,
Defenseless as the quail flushed from its nest,
    Waiting to be shot.

The force of all the Colonies combines
    To overwhelm.
There's Benjamin Church out in the field
    And casting wide
His net made tight with captured Indians,
    Who must agree
To serve him as his soldiers—or it's
    The ships or death!
Each day more and more, war-weary, submit
    Without a shot,
And the starving surrender in numbers at
    Boston and Plymouth.
Others drift north, hoping to make it out
    Of the country.

When Philip's uncle, Akkompoin, is killed
    At Titicut,
Our wives and children taken. . . . Oh, we
    Are broken men!
All of the fire gone out of the heart,
    Yet we fight on.
And when our Sachem's head is on a pole
    At Plymouth,
And Weetamoo's the same, displayed on
    Taunton Green,

And Quinnapin, her husband, tried and shot
    At Newport,
And we, beyond all doubt, have lost our country,
    Still we fight on.
Then Church sends word that I might have my life
    And save my family
From the slave ships, if now, with Philip dead,
    I will come in.
I think on this . . . and hear across the stillness
    The owl call my name.

Amie: Mionie

Did you know of my late husband, Tuspaquin,
      What they did to him?
I am his wife, Mionie. It is the Whites,
      Who have no ear
For Indian names, have called me Amie.
      But I would have you
Know me as Aquene: in our language
      It means peace—
Peace, the heart's own wish. And peace was what
      My father,
That good man Massasoit—Ousamequin—
      Honored most.
Through all the days of his long life he strove
      To nurture peace
Between the tribes, and with our people
      And the English.

I was, my parents said, the quiet one,
      The peaceful one,
Papoose that never cried, except when
      Needing to be fed.
The one who would play hours at a time
      Peacefully alone
With pebbles and shells, feathers of the
      Tanager and jay . . .
In little games I made up for myself,
      So long ago.
Then war was but a tale the warriors told,
      And no more real
Than when the old ones gathered round the fire
      And lit the pipe

And fed the blaze an offering of tobacco,
      And someone
Sat erect and cleared his throat, and all grew still
      And hunched in close,
Knowing what was coming was a story.
      Ah! word pictures
Of spirits and demons and sky people;
      Tales of old Squant,
Of her children and husband, the man-giant
      Maushop,
Who dwelt inside an old fire-mountain hole
      And smoked his pipe
Of stone, with which he made new land spring up
      Out of the ocean.
One day he said, I'll make a place where Indians
      May light their fires,
Hunt animals for food and skins, build wetus
      For their homes.
He waded out with his stone pipe beyond
      His knees and thighs
And knocked it on a rock upon the ocean floor.
      And there, right there
Where all the ashes in a heap fell out,
      New land sprang up,
With waterfalls and streams, plants and trees and
      Every growing thing.
And when Great Spirit looked around and saw
      That it was good,
He put our people here, with animals,
      And all you see.

Uncle Akkompoin—who died at Titicut
      Defending us—

Would take his pipe and puff on it, pretending
    To be Maushop. . . .
It soothes my heart when I think back upon
    Those childhood days.
And if it's true I seldom cried when young,
    Well, I weep now,
When each day brings another death to mourn,
    Another sorrow from
The hand we welcomed with the hand of peace:
    What cheer, netop?
Netop: friend. —When was the Whiteman ever
    Our true friend?
Kemineiachick: murderers—is more
    The truth of it.
Have you heard about my husband, Tuspaquin,
    What they did to him?
—The broken pledge, the sham by which
    They slew him?
When Captain Church had promised safety
    For him and family
If he would peacefully submit now that
    Metacom was dead.

I will tell you how the men of Plymouth
    Mocked my husband,
Mocked his station as powwaw and *pniese:*
    His warrior power.
Saying, as his medicine was known
    To be so strong
No bullet ever touched him, they would have
    The proof of it.
Thus, with Captain Church away at Boston,
    They lay hold of him

And shot him, scoffing how Black Sachem
      Did fall down dead
When bullets struck, like any mortal man.
      The wretches next
Shot Annawon, chief counselor to Philip,
      To my father
And brother before him; Annawon was
      Family to me.
For all his years the proud old man stood tall
      And straight as a tree
On which the snows of winter lightly rest:
      A modest man
Of courage and honor, wise and strong,
      And true of heart.
Most noble in defeat he was, and this
      We know as told
By Church, the Englishman, and since repeated
      To my ears,
How War Captain Annawon, with great and
      Solemn dignity
Surrendered up the wampum belts and all
      The grand regalia,
Insignia of office that was Philip's.
      This, in formal
Recognition that the war was lost and
      Thus acknowledged
By this act, that they might make an end
      To bloodshed then.

An end to bloodshed? . . . A ghastly end for
      All my family,
For Annawon, Tuspaquin, Metacom—
      Massasoit's son!

Noble men that thirsted after justice,
    Their severed heads
Displayed upon a palisade in Plymouth
    To public mockery,
By such as were so helpless when first they
    Came among us.
Now, in the triumph of their stolen power,
    So pitiless.

Gone: Metacom, Tuspaquin, Annawon . . .
    Names in the wind.
Brother, husband, friend—gone! Valiant men,
    Heart of a nation.
And the spark they lit—that caught, and flared
    And spread
In every patriot breast—snuffed: that hope
    But scattered ash.

I would share with you this dream, this vision
    That came to him,
My husband, troubling and consoling, before
    The war began.
He saw himself pursued and fleeing from
    The English,
When he heard a voice gentle but strong that
    Bade him, *Come!*
And then it was as if he had been lifted
    High above,
And looking down beheld the great salt sea,
    And floating there
A tortoise huge, greater than an island,
    Grandfather,
He was sure, of all tortoises that ever were.
    And upon its back

He saw a struggle going on between
    The races,
Red and White, a fierce and bloody contest;
    It sickened him.
He saw the Redmen fall, the Whites prevail
    And take possession.
And everywhere upon the back of that
    Great creature
He saw blood, and then as sudden as a
    Wind comes up
He saw the mighty tortoise dive down deep,
    Far out of sight
And cleanse itself then surface to the light,
    Washed clean of blood
And Whitemen, and gone were all their works.
    Oh, naught was left
Of cow or plow, no trace or sign they had
    Ever been at all!
Then came a great horned owl and from its beak
    Fell many seeds
Until the tortoise back was covered well
    In every part
With growing things of plant and fur and fin.
    And then once more
He heard the spirit voice, gentle and strong,
    Addressing him:
"The blown flower's seed returns to earth to wait
    The season of rebirth.
What is shall pass, what was shall come again,
    Take heart, O Sachem."

This dream, this prophecy shall live when I
    And mine are gone.

And he who put us on this earth to be
    And do his will,
The one who seeing, sees all, that great one
    Who dwells beyond,
Shall in his own time by his own means fulfill
    The prophecy,
This dream, this vision of Tuspaquin—
    Hope of Metacom. . . .
This I do believe, for this I pray
    With my last breath.
Great Spirit, hear the one who calls to you
    In peace, Aquene.

NB: It remains unresolved whether Amie and Mionie were one and the same daughter of Massasoit, or two separate individuals. I am persuaded they were a single individual, by the fact of her brothers having taken English names, and from the similarity of sound. If this is not the case, any other Wampanoag name for Amie is lost to posterity. Aquene, meaning "peace," is the author's attribution, taken from the Natick Dictionary, Bureau of American Ethnology, 1903.

Taunton Agreement

Taunton, April 10th, 1671.

Whereas my Father, my Brother, and my self, have formally submitted ourselves and our People unto the Kings Majesty of England, and to the Colony of New Plimouth, by solemn Covenant under our Hand; but I having of late through my Indiscretion, and the Naughtiness of my Heart, violated and broken this my Covenant with my Friends, by taking up Arms, with evil intent against them, and that groundlessly; I being now deeply sensible of my Unfaithfulness and Folly, do desire at this Time solemnly to renew my Covenant with my ancient Friends, and my Fathers Friends above mentioned, and do desire that this may testify to the World against me if ever I shall again fail in my Faithfulness towards them (that I have now, and at all Times found so kind to me) or any other of the English Colonies; and as a real Pledge of my true Intentions for the Future to be Faithful and Friendly, I do freely engage to resign up unto the Government of New Plimouth, all my English Arms, to be kept by them for their Security, so long as they shall see Reason. For true Performance of the Premises, I have hereunto set my Hand, together with the Rest of my Council.

In Presence of

    William Davis.

    William Hudson.

    Thomas Brattle.

        The Mark of **P.** *Philip*,

            Chief Sachem of *Pocanoket.*

        The Mark of **V** *Tavoser.*

        The Mark of **M** *Capt. Wisposke.*

        The Mark of **T** *Woonkaponehunt.*

        The Mark of **8** *Nimrod.*

Glossary

Cowwewonck	The spirit or soul.
Iootash	Stand firm and fight.
Kautantowwit	God of the southwest, from which good things come, and where it is hoped the soul will go after death.
Manit, manitto; plural, manittowock (Variant: manito, manitoo, manitou, etc.)	A god or spirit.
Netop	Friend.
Pniese (paniese)	Man of valor, esteemed warrior, who it was believed could not be killed in battle.
Powwaw (powwow)	Priest, medicine man, shaman.
Saunks	Queen, sachem's wife.
Wampanoag	The people of the first light, of the eastern shore.
Wetu	The traditional, dome-shaped dwelling of the region, covered with mats and/or skins. "Wigwam" is the more familiar corruption of this word.
Wuttamauog	Tobacco.
Yotaanit	God of fire.

Indian Place and Tribal Names

Agawam – Springfield, Massachusetts.

Asquash (Ashquoach: Old Quabaug Fort) –
    Brimfield, MA.

Assawompsett – Middleborough/Lakeville, MA.

Assawompsett Pond – Lakeville, MA.

Cocheco – Dover, New Hampshire.

Great Swamp Fort – South Kingston, Rhode Island.

Hassanamesit – Praying Town, Grafton, MA.

Mahican – New York tribe at Schaghticoke,
    north of Albany (occasionally confused
    with Connecticut Mohegan).

Menemesit (Menameset, Wenimisset) – So. Barre/
    New Braintree, MA.

Mohawk – Iroquoian tribe of New York and
    Canada, feared as war-like.

Mohegan – Central to eastern Connecticut; allied
    themselves with the English.

Monponsett Pond – Halifax, MA.

Montaup (Mt. Hope) – Bristol, RI: Philip's seat.

Narragansett – Principle Rhode Island tribe.

Nashaway – Lancaster, MA.

Natick – Praying Town, Natick, MA.

Nemasket – Middleborough, MA.

Niantic – Southeastern CT and RI; related to the
    Narragansett. (Western Niantic were a
    separate branch, subject to the Pequot, who
    had established themselves on the Thames
    River, dividing the Niantic into two groups.
    After the Pequot War, 1637, they were
    under the Mohegan.)

Nipmuck – West central MA into CT. Nashaway/
    Weshakim, Nipmuck, Quabaug, and
    Wabaquasset tribes are generally grouped
    together as Nipmuck or Nipmuck Country.

Nipsachuck Swamp – Smithfield, RI.

Norwottuck – Hadley/Northampton, MA.

Pakachoog – Praying Town near Millbury, MA.

Pawtucket Falls – Blackstone River, RI.

Pawtuckett/Pennacook – Northeastern MA into southern New Hampshire.

Pequot – Central CT, seated at Thames River. An aggressive regional power until the 1637 war left them subject to the Mohegan.

Peskeompscut – Turners Falls, Montague, MA.

Pocasset – Fall River, MA/Tiverton, RI.

Pocumtuck – Deerfield, MA, Conn. River Valley.

Pokanoket – Bristol, RI: Philip's primary locus.

Pokanoket/Wampanoag – (See Wampanoag Fed.).

Quabaug – North Brookfield, MA.

Quinsigamond – Worcester, MA.

Sakonnet – Little Compton, RI.

Schaghticoke – North of Albany, NY, on Hoosic R.

Squakeag – Northfield, MA.

Squannakonk Swamp – Rehoboth, MA.

Squinnicook (Squnnicook) – Groton, MA.

Squinshepauke (Quishapauge) – Mendon, MA.

Titicut – Bridgewater/North Middleborough, MA.

Titicut River – Taunton River, MA.

Wabaquasset – Woodstock, CT.

Wachusett Mt. – Princeton, MA.

Wamesit – Praying Town, near Lowell, MA.

Wampanoag Federation – Southeastern MA to eastern RI and Cape Cod, with wide-ranging influence.

Wannamoisett – Barrington, RI.

Weshakim – Sterling, MA.

Wessagusset – Weymouth, MA.

Note: Most New England tribes were named for some geographic feature of their location, which may lead to confusion. For example, Agawam, of which there were three known villages of that name in Massachusetts alone, at Ipswich, Springfield, and Wareham.

A Note to the Reader

From the bibliography assembled in my research for *Voices of King Philip's War,* I would recommend the following as a good starting point for those interested in pursuing the subject further.

Connole, Dennis A. *The Indians of the Nipmuck Country in Southern New England 1630-1750.* North Carolina and London: McFarland & Co., 2001. This book is a major contribution to our knowledge of the various central Massachusetts Algonquian communities loosely grouped as Nipmuck; an invaluable source of information on these tribes, who initially played such a pivotal role in propelling the war forward, and later in hastening its end.

Leach, Douglas Edward. *Flintlock and Tomahawk: New England in King Philip's War.* New York: W. W. Norton, 1966. This is the book I credit with launching me on the fascinating exploration of this defining episode in our nation's history. Originally published in 1958, the book maintains its place as one of the best chronicles of the conflict available. Its helpful bibliography served me well as a reliable guide in pursuing my own research.

Lepore, Jill. *The Name of War: King Philip's War and the Origins of American Identity.* New York: Vintage Press, 1999. Lepore provides an insightful analysis and cautionary study of the cultural biases and conflicting values that made inevitable the clash between colonist and Indian, erupting as King Philip's War. She examines the subject through the lens of language, the written word vs. oral tradition, underscoring the critical role literacy, or the lack thereof, played in shaping the course of events and the interpretation of them offered to posterity.

Lincoln, Charles H., ed. *Narratives of the Indian Wars 1675-1699. (Original Narratives of the Early American History* Series, 1913). Reprint. New York: Barnes & Noble, Inc., 1966. I include this useful anthology of early documents for those who wish to acquaint themselves with some of the contemporary writings on the war. Inaccuracies found in the original reportage are noted by the editor.

Philbrick, Nathaniel. *Mayflower.* London: Penguin Books, 2007. Philbrick's award winning book is an engaging, comprehensive view of English settlement in colonial America from its European beginnings to the flashpoint of King Philip's War. It is packed with information, well-researched, and reads with the engrossing quality of a novel.

Schultz, Eric B. and Michael J. Tougias. *King Philip's War: The History and Legacy of America's Forgotten Conflict.* Woodstock, VT: Countryman Press, 2000. This collaborative work is a richly detailed, updated chronicle of the war, with extensive illustrations, maps and photographs of conflict sites. Also included are excerpts from diaries and eyewitness accounts. This painstaking study is a valuable contribution to our knowledge of that neglected period in our history, and it serves as a useful guidebook to the loci of those dramatic events.

Acknowledgments

I wish to acknowledge those who have so gener-
ously given of their time, talents, and encourage-
ment in the preparation of *Voices of King Philip's
War:*

My heartfelt thanks to Winston Bolton, dear friend
and keen copy editor, who proofread each success-
ive draft, offering valuable critical insights and
catching typos along the way.

I am enormously indebted to Dr. Daniel Hoffman
for his openhearted encouragement of my creative
efforts over the years; and more immediately, for
the wise counsel and fresh insights which have
aided me greatly in the revision process of *Voices.*

And to Janet Locke, for her expertise, tireless super-
vision, and angelic patience in guiding manuscript
preparation every step of the way, I owe the suc-
cessful completion of all technical aspects of this
project.

Thank you all.

Author photo by Winston F. Bolton

FAYE GEORGE

Faye George's published collections include *A Wound On Stone,* winner of the 2001 Perugia Press Prize, *Back Roads* (Rock Village Publishing, 2003), *Märchenhaft,* (Earthwinds Editions, 2008); and chapbooks *Only The Words* (1995), and *Naming The Place: The Weymouth Poems* (1996). The latter is a nostalgic tribute to the town where the author was born and raised. Weymouth, the Wessagusset of 1622, bordered Wampanoag lands to the northeast. It was within the jurisdiction of the Massachusetts under the sachem Chickataubut, who died of smallpox in 1633.

George's poems have appeared in numerous distinguished publications, university press periodicals, and anthologies: *The Paris Review, Poetry,* and *Poetry's* 90th year retrospective, *The Poetry Anthology, 1912-2002; The Anthology of Magazine Verse and Yearbook of American Poetry; Poetry Daily,* and others. Her work has been profiled in *The Boston Globe* and *The Providence Journal,* and featured online with *Agni, The Cultural Society, The Endicott Journal of Mythic Arts,* and *Poetry Daily.*

She has received the Arizona Poetry Society's Memorial Award, and the New England Poetry Club's Gretchen Warren Award and Erika Mumford Prize.

Faye George has worked as copywriter, public relations representative, and academic secretary. She is now retired and living in Bridgewater, Massachusetts.

CPSIA information can be obtained at www.ICGtesting.com
Printed in the USA
LVOW081849090413

328363LV00012B/1380/P